WOMEN of COLOR
DAILY DEVOTIONAL

JUNE - JULY - AUGUST

JUNE
WEEK ONE: MARRIAGE

DAY 1
I Wish, I Wish, I Wish

HAPPINESS...

"The trying of your faith worketh patience.
But let patience have her perfect work,
that ye may be perfect and entire, wanting nothing.
If any of you lack wisdom, let him ask of God,
that giveth to all men liberally, and upbraideth not;
and it shall be given him."

JAMES 1:3-5

A woman and her husband were approaching their tenth wedding anniversary. It had been a hard ten years. Soft, loving words were long absent from their conversations. Their intimate times were few and far between and were mechanical. Neither really knew if the other was being faithful, and if the truth be told, neither really cared. They avoided talking about important things like feelings and dreams because each of them regularly invalidated what the other was thinking and feeling. Mostly, their conversations led to degrading remarks, name-calling, accusations, and arguments that sometimes turned physical.

They both professed to love the Lord and were outspoken at Bible studies and the like. But neither knew the depth of faith the other had because they never shared their faith on an intimate level. They'd tried going to a marriage counselor but it didn't work and just gave them more ammunition to argue.

She'd gotten to the point where she couldn't watch another couple walk down the street holding hands or looking lovingly at each other, let alone watch a romantic movie, without crying. A happy marriage was no longer a hope or prayer. Now she would settle for a civil relationship with her material needs met. But when she was alone with God, she wondered (but dared not ask God), Is this all that you have for me?

APPLICATION

The difference between maturity and immaturity is the difference between acting on what we know instead of acting on what we feel. All of us want to be happy. But we must learn to differentiate between fleeting moments of feeling happy and lasting joy and fulfillment. Feelings can be very deceptive and can change very quickly. On the other hand, true, lasting joy that comes from the Lord, increases our faith, brings joy and teaches us perseverance (James 1:2-3). When we recognize that we are like mighty oaks whose roots run deep (Isaiah 61:3); we won't sway in the wind from one emotion to the next. Instead, we learn to look beyond our circumstances and realize that joy is found in trusting God , because we look beyond the circumstances. We know that each of us is a work in progress and that, just as labor pains, whatever we are going through will birth us anew, greater and mightier, stronger and happier than before. The Lord invites us to partake in this kind of joy in him. We can have it whenever we choose. Today, right this moment. Enter into the joy of the Lord (Matthew 25:21, 23).

Try spreading joy. It's infectious. Try going through a whole day saying nothing but words of encouragement to other people and with nothing but a pleasant expression. No negative body language. Respond to negativism around you with love and positive statements. Find the positive in every situation and express it to those around you. It doesn't matter if you feel it. Just do it. By the end of the day you will be energized, at peace, and truly smiling from the inside out.

PRAYER

Lord, in you I can find true joy and happiness. You came to teach me that. And if I find happiness in you, then I do not need to find happiness in my marriage. Yet if I am filled with your joy, I will fill my home with joy also. Lord, give me your joy to renew my marriage and restore the places in it that have been devastated. I pray, Amen.

DAY 2

What's Love Got to Do with It?

LOVE...

*"And now abideth faith, hope,
charity, these three; but the greatest of these is charity."*
1CORINTHIANS 13:13

There was a young couple that when they were first married, they were all over each other—couldn't get enough kissin' and huggin' and showing love to one another. Being in each other's presence was exhilarating; it was easy as breathing air. The first year of marriage they hit a few bumps. She realized that he snored all night and passed gas loudly, not caring who was around. He realized she was an unorganized, messy housekeeper. Until they married, she never realized how critical and nit-picky he was; and he realized that she was a bit of a gossip.

About six months into the marriage, she was pregnant with their first child. Immediately, his belly began to grow, just like hers. After the baby arrived, neither of them got back to their pre-baby weight. She was forgiving of his weight gain, but he kept nagging her about not being the brick house that he married. Arguments ensued as did some nights of sleeping in separate bedrooms. Now, at the end of the second year of marriage, the thrill seemed gone. They were both wondering if continuing the marriage was a good idea.

APPLICATION

The Love chapter of 1 Corinthians 13 has been read at scores of weddings to describe the endurance of marital love. The truth is, it describes the endurance of God's love. We cannot begin to understand the depth of God's love until we meet him face to face. On that day, all other things will be gone and probably forgotten, but God, who is love, will be left, along with the faith and hope we will see in him.

We are only poor imitators of God's love, but we must always strive to be more like him. We must live a life of love, just as Christ loved us and gave himself up for us (Ephesians 5:1, 2). Some of us have to go back and learn what love is because the love we learned from our families didn't come close to God's love. God's love is patient, kind, not envious, doesn't boast, and is not proud. God is not easily angered, keeps no record of wrongs, and doesn't delight in evil but rejoices in truth. God's love always protects, trusts, hopes and perseveres. God's love never fails (1 Corinthians 13:4-8). This does not describe a feeling but a relationship built upon God's Word. If your marriage is built on this kind of love, God's love, it will endure when all else fails.

Each day make sure that you commit an act of love toward your husband. It doesn't have to be a big gesture. The act of making love doesn't count. It can just be to listen to him without speaking, give him a card, a hug, a touch, or maybe just a nice look or a warm smile. How about cook his favorite meal?

PRAYER

Lord, I want to be more like you. I want to be able to say that about my love for my husband. Convict me when I judge him. Help us to be best friends, lovers, and admirers of each other. Lord, I know that no matter how far my marriage is from that now, that your Word promises me blessings if I am obedient to you. Lord, I ask for your blessings upon my marriage in the name of Jesus, Amen.

DAY 3

How committed am I?

OBEDIENCE...

"Therefore take heed to your spirit,
and let none deal treacherously
against the wife of his youth."

MALACHI 2:15

Letricia had suffered much embarrassment by her husband, Jamie. Over and over again he had misused their finances. Cars had been repossessed in front of the neighbors, credit cards declined at business lunches, and calls received about foreclosure on their house. All of this, because Jamie refused to contribute his full paycheck to take care of household responsibilities. It was his point of view that he worked too hard to have all his money go toward bills.

Somehow he always avoided dealing with the repercussions of his carelessness, and it was Letricia who got the phone calls from the bill collectors. He was viewed as the big man among his friends. He was always picking up the tab or peeling off a twenty to give to somebody. It's like his manhood was tied up in how big a wad of bills he had in his pocket.

APPLICATION

We are not commanded in God's Word to marry, but once we do, God says that we are united to our spouse and will become one flesh (Genesis 2:24). This is not a temporary arrangement, but a lifelong covenant that we voluntarily enter into before God. Marriage is the first relationship God made after our relationship with him. We are committed to our marriages because we are obedient to the Word of God, and we take our direction from him. There's no need for us to struggle with a decision (maybe I'll stay, maybe I'll go), if the answer is in his Word.

Now don't misunderstand. Being obedient does not mean that you remain with a man who is abusing you. Separation may be necessary when physical or sexual misuse is involved. Remove yourself and get help.

But the truth is that God hates divorce (Malachi 2:16) and commands us not to separate. If we do separate, the goal should be reconciliation or remaining alone (1 Corinthians 7:10). You may not be at such a desperate crossroads but you may see the signs.

Do you want to improve your marriage? Work with God on it. Do you really want more quality time with your husband? Work with God to get it. Do you really want to grow in the Lord with your spouse? Work with God to get it.

Read Ephesians chapter 5 and make a list of the ways the chapter tells you to behave in your marriage. Ask yourself each day if you have carried out what is on that list.

PRAYER

Lord, I stand upon your Word. I know that it is your will for me to remain married to my husband. But there are issues. Lord, show me how to deal with those issues according to your Word. You, oh Lord, are my strength and my Redeemer. Amen.

DAY 4

Prayer Changes Things

PRAYER...

*"And shall not God avenge his own elect,
which cry day and night unto him,
though he bear long with them? I
tell you that he will avenge them speedily."*

LUKE 18:8

Before they got married, Alicia and Oliver went through six weeks of pre-marital counseling. They wanted to enter into this thing together. It didn't take long, however, before Oliver began to stay home from church in favor of a game, a movie, or just to get some sleep. Alicia got tired of going to church alone and thought that if she could just get his butt in the pew, he'd hear the message and be motivated to return to church. She nagged and nagged, which caused argument after argument. Pretty soon, the subject of

church, let alone the subject of God, was banned from their conversation.

Alicia recognized that this separateness was not what God wanted for their marriage. So, she decided that perhaps the answer was to stay home with him on the weekends...just for a while. If this church thing is a problem, she'll just cool out on going for just a bit. This will also give her an opportunity to witness to him and his friends.

APPLICATION

You can't change your husband, nor should you desire to change him. It would be scary what most husbands would be if we did have the power to change them. Don't misunderstand, don't ever stay in the presence of abuse. But who your husband is and what he will be is between him and God. It is not your place to judge your husband (James 4:11). God may use you as an instrument your husband's life, but you are not the changer, God is. You are not responsible for your husband's relationship with the Lord. The more you think you are taking control of the situation, the more you may be the instrument for the enemy to harden your husband's heart.

When was the last time you prayed for your husband? Every time you come before the Lord to pray about anything, you should pray for your husband. Put aside at least one time a day to pray for nothing and nobody but your husband. Complaining about him accomplishes nothing, but your righteous prayers are powerful and effective (James 5:16). Pick a time that can become an easy routine, such as when you take your shower or when you are in your car on the way to work. Pray that this day he will have a clear path and a double portion of blessings. The next day pray that he will have discernment and patience as he goes about his work. Intercede for him when he has an important business meeting. Pray blessings over him. Bind the enemy from touching his life. Pray joy over his life. Remember, no complaining about him. Just lift him up for the Lord to bless.

PRAYER

Lord, help me to remember to pray for my husband. Whether he is a believer or not, I need to pray for him. Help me to find a time to do that. Help me to remember to mention him first in my prayers. And Lord, remind me every day that I cannot change him. Let me pray silently about the things that I would change. Let me truly release these things to you so that I do not keep bringing them up to him. Amen.

DAY 5

All Things Are Possible

FAITH...

*"If ye have faith as a grain of mustard seed,
ye shall say unto this mountain,
Remove hence to yonder place; and it shall remove;
and nothing shall be impossible unto you."*

MATTHEW 17:20

Della had been waiting on the Lord for a husband. She met a man whom she felt sure was the right one and married him. But not soon after the marriage the trouble started Della was steadfast, and for years she waited on the Lord to heal her marriage. While she was "waiting on the Lord," she kept trying herself to fix what was wrong with her husband. Nothing worked. At her wit's end, she fell on her face before the Lord and gave the burden to him. The Lord showed her that she could not fix anything and that she should let him fight her battles. She had done this before and picked the burden back up when she got off her knees, but this time she was obedient and left it at the altar.

She stayed in prayer for her husband. She honored her husband and was obedient to what the Word says a wife should be. She worked on her relationship with Christ and humbled herself before him. She let him search her to fix the brokenness in her. As she wrestled with her obedience, it got easier and easier to do what God said to do.

Years later she realized that somewhere along the way everything started working again. She and her husband were in ministry together. They'd never been closer or more "in love." She couldn't tell you when it actually came back together again. All she could remember was the day that she laid it down before God and left it there.

APPLICATION

Do you believe that God has a plan and purpose for your life? Just because you can't see the great work that God is doing doesn't mean that he isn't doing it. Just because you can't understand what God is doing doesn't mean that it's not part of his plan and purpose to bless you.

Whenever you are afraid, anxious, worried, desperate, irritated, or angry, or you've stopped having faith that God can do what he said he'd do. You've got to have faith enough to let God be God in your life and trust that he is always in control.

Many problems of faith are due to the presence of fear—fear that something will or will not occur. Treat fear like the demon it is and exorcise it whenever it appears. When you feel worried or anxious, clarify it. "I am afraid that..." Then say to yourself, Where there is fear, there is no faith. The two cannot occupy the same space. Use the power of Jesus over fear to cast it out in his name.

PRAYER

Lord, I want to be the woman of God that you called me to be. I want to be the wife to my husband that you've called me to be. Lord, cleanse my heart and mend the broken places in my life that keep me from being all that I can be in you. I trust in you, Lord, with all my heart. Amen.

JUNE
WEEK TWO: HUSBANDS

DAY 1
Pray for Your Husband

LORD GET HIM!

"And he spake a parable unto them to this end,
that men ought always to pray, and not to faint."
LUKE 18:1

Kneeling with her prayer partner, a godly older woman, Melissa began to pray, "Lord, make my husband more sensible and, Lord, get him for the rude remarks he made about me at dinner yesterday. Lord, could you make him a better Sunday School teacher so the class will be more exciting? My husband really needs your blessings in the name of Jesus I pray, Amen."

As Melissa rose from her knees, her prayer partner said in a loving way "Now, let's pray

for your husband." Melissa, like so many other wives, had begun to pray on her husband instead of praying for him.

It is easy to fall into a practice of rehearsing our partners' faults during prayer rather than praying for their needs and their walk with God. Luke 18:1 says we ought always to pray and not faint. What does it mean to faint? It means giving in to the flesh, responding to situations. We must fight the urge to give in to our selfish desires even when we pray! One simple way to avoid the temptation to voice our selfish desires is to simply pray using God's own words in Scripture.

APPLICATION

Today when you pray for your husband, choose to bless him and build his character in prayer. Choose a Scripture with promise and pray that Scripture into his life. Watch God be true to his Word and perform it.

PRAYER

Father God, today I come lifting up my husband, a man after God's own heart. Father, I pray that my husband shall know the truth and the truth shall make him free (John 8:32). Lord, I pray that my husband will cast his care upon you, for you care for him (1 Peter 5:7). In the name of Jesus I pray, Amen.

DAY 2

Serving Your Husband

OH! THOSE BEAUTIFUL FEET...

"And whatsoever ye do, do it heartily, as to the Lord, and not unto men."

COLOSSIANS 3:23

The story is told of a family out for an afternoon drive. Dad notices his little girl standing up in the back seat of the car. Dad says, "Cindy, sit down," but Cindy continues to stand. Dad says again in a much firmer tone, "Cindy, I said sit down!" Finally, Cindy sits.

Cindy then looks at her dad with tears in her eyes and declares, "I'm still standing up in my heart!"

Ladies, many wives today, when they hear the words serve and husband in the same sentence react much like Cindy. We serve, but our hearts are not in it. I believe that our husbands know when our serving is not from the heart.

APPLICATION

Realize there is no limelight in serving. Often service is overlooked. Depend on the Spirit of God to fill you with the ability to carry out your daily duties without a pat on the back. Search the Scriptures and see how many examples of service the Bible records. Jesus said, "I come into the world to serve not to be served." Serving in the beginning will be awkward but the more you serve, the more natural it will come to you. Serving will go against the grain, but remember that with Christ we can do all things. Finally, Jesus said he who wants to be the greatest must be the servant of all. Ladies, that also means in our marriages. Imagine you can be the greatest wife there is—not through good looks, not through perfection, but through service! What a blessing. That levels the playing field, doesn't it? It matters not whether you are a new bride or a seasoned bride you can still be the greatest wife through service.

Serving means more than just giving your husband the things he asks for, it also means developing a vision about what he wants and needs and even what he likes. To accomplish this, you must study him and know his moods and habits. Take note at what brings a smile to his face.

Picking up around the house is a big act of service that can become an issue. Try this exercise next time you see your husband's dirty socks in the middle of the floor: As you pick them up one more time, instead of grumbling just pray this prayer: "Oh those beautiful feet, Lord, I thank you for him. Lord, I bless every place his feet shall trod today." After a while an opportunity for prayer has developed from an act that used to bring on a source of resentment. Serving with gladness is possible. Change your attitude and your servitude will change also.

P R A Y E R

Father, in the name of Jesus, the greatest example of a servant, help me to become aware of opportunities to serve my husband. Help me serve with gladness. Lord, give me the spirit you had when you washed the disciples feet. I want to model you in every area of my life including serving. In your name I pray, Amen.

DAY 3

Obey Your Husband

MAN OVER MATTER, NOT MATTER OVER YOUR MAN...

"To be discreet, chaste, keepers at home, good, obedient to their own husbands, that the Word of God be not blasphemed."

TITUS 2:5

Shirley heard a knock at her door. She recognized her friend Brenda's voice and let her in. "Brenda, what's wrong with you?"

Brenda wiped away a tear. "I don't know. Lately Preston and I have not been getting along. We argue all the time."

31

"What do you argue about?"

"I just want him to try harder to see things my way. I am a professional woman. I run a major business with several employees, but he thinks I can't manage our home and finances as well. Why should I do things the way Preston wants me to? He takes too long to reach a decision, for one thing. Really, Shirley, I don't know if I can live like this much longer."

Shirley took a breath to let emotions settle. "Brenda, Titus 2:5 says we are to be discreet, chaste keepers at home, and obedient to our husbands. You are not to be obedient to your husband because he outwits you or because you are incapable of taking care of business, but because the Word of God has given headship to the man. Submit yourself to God and your husband and see the arguments stop. Depend on God to bless your marriage and your husband."

After a moment's thought, Brenda said, "Thank you, Shirley. I suppose I have brought my work position into my home. I didn't realize that's what I was doing. I'm going to strive to allow my man to rule over matter and not rule over him through my actions."

APPLICATION

As we submit our wills to God and then our husbands, we will see the hand of God direct our husbands in the headship of our families. Two people cannot be the head at the same time. Walk together and lean on your husband. Don't expect him to lean on you.

The secret to obedience is to realize that God has given you the power to obey. Don't be afraid that you will be taken advantage of. 1 Peter 3:1 says that wives should be in subjection to their husbands. 1 Corinthians 11:3 says that Christ is the head of the man, and the man is the head of the woman. Write down today concrete ways in which you can act on those Scriptures at home.

PRAYER

Father God, in the name of Jesus I desire to be an obedient wife. I pray that I would be a wife that submits herself to her own husband as unto the Lord, for the husband is the head of the wife. In Jesus name, Amen.

DAY 4

Encourage Your Husband

OFF HIS BACK AND IN HIS FACE...

"It is better to dwell in a corner of a housetop than with a brawling woman in a wide house."

PROVERBS 21:9

Two small bodies huddled together in the corner of the kitchen as they watched Dad and Mom yelling to the top of their lungs again. The children's cries began to get the attention of their father, Rob. He looked in their direction and then stormed out of the house. Mom Amanda just sat where she was wondering what she would do this time. How had their marriage come to this? Amanda wanted to hurt Rob. Everything in her just wanted to lash out. She felt out of

control. What frightened her the most was that she didn't know if she could get herself under control.

Amanda sat in her pastor's office the next morning alone. Rob had not come home that night. Upon explaining to her pastor her fits of anger and even physical altercations with her husband the pastor lead her in prayer and to a Scripture about the danger of anger. Shortly after that, Amanda entered an anger management class and she and Rob began marital counseling.

APPLICATION

When you are tempted to get on your husband's back about some things he has not done, or some business he did not take care of, decide instead to get off his back and in his face with words of encouragement. In other words, build him up instead of tearing him down. Every morning choose a different Scripture that builds up and make that the Scripture of the day. Speak that word into his life all day instead of negativity. The world tears our men down enough. They need to know someone is in their corner. Become a place of refuge, an oasis in the desert of life. Write down the Scripture and keep it before you. Philippians 4:8 says, "Finally, brethren, whatsoever things are true, whatsoever things are honest, whatsoever things are just, whatsoever things are pure, whatsoever things are lovely, whatsoever things are of good report; if there be any virtue, and if there be any praise, think on these things."

To jump start your practice of affirmation and encouragement to your husband, here is a little exercise that gets big results.

Every time you want to get on his back about something, stop in your tracks, stop in mid-sentence, and get in his face with a nice kiss. Then say your word for the day that will encourage him. What a change you will see right away! First there will be a change in you: The words of affirmation will cause you to see your husband in a different light. You have the ability to choose your reaction to every situation.

PRAYER

Lord God, I submit to you my impatience and my desire to rule over my husband. Father, forgive me for the short temper and even the physical fights that I have initiated with my spouse. Through your Spirit I know it can be right again. In the name of Jesus I pray, Amen.

DAY 5

Love Your Husband

WHAT'S LOVE GOT TO DO WITH IT?

"[Love] doth not behave itself unseemly, seeketh not her own, is not easily provoked, thinketh no evil."

1 CORINTHIANS 13:5

Janet had begun to see every fault in Ed. Everything he said was wrong. She wondered as she stared at him across the breakfast table: Why did I ever marry him? Ed, having sensed for quite some time that something was wrong, asked Janet, "Do you still love me?"

Janet thought for a moment then responded, "I believe I do, but what does love have to do with the way I feel now?"

Ed, remembering how they used to pray together, invited Janet to pray with him. Afterward Janet did feel better. When Janet told the story to her sister Donnie, Donnie asked, "Janet do you pray for Ed everyday as you used to? To pray for him is to bless him. Pray for his needs. When you see him, remember he is your love, your life-long partner. Janet, don't base your marriage on a feeling. Stop asking yourself how you feel and affirm to yourself that you are in love and trust that your marriage will glorify God.

APPLICATION

Wives must remember that marriage is not all romance. Husbands must deal with our shortcomings just as we must deal with their shortcomings. The Bible says love bears all things, believes all things, hopes all things, endures all things. This gives us the only true definition of love. With Christ and with prayer we can maintain a heart of love for our husbands.

When you begin to see shortcomings in your husband, remember that he is still the man you married. Remember that love has everything to do with your relationship with him and pray earnestly for him. Love never fails.

Get a journal and call it your love journal. Write down all the things you love about your husband. Put in some of your favorite pictures of him and some of the notes he has written to you. Every day record something he has done that day that expresses his love for you. Don't look for big things. Look for the little things that you have started to take for granted, the things that say, "Honey, I still love you."

PRAYER

Father, in the name of Jesus you said in your Word that God is love. Father, I desire to love my husband and respect him. I want to honor our marriage. Take away my heart of stone and give me a heart of flesh. In Jesus name I pray, Amen.

JUNE
WEEK THREE: DIVORCE

DAY 1

Be Careful What You Pray For!

THINKING ABOUT DIVORCE?

*"Delight thyself also in the Lord;
and he shall give thee the desires of thine heart."*

PSALM 37:4

As she sipped her fourth glass of wine, Georgette's mind began to wander. When she was a little girl, she dreamed of being married and having a man she could love and take care of and vice versa. She remembered being 25 and impatient to find Mr. Right. That's when she began praying daily that God would send her a mate because church and the bar scene just weren't serving her needs. Then Daniel suddenly

appeared in her life, and Georgette believed her prayers had been answered. He said and did all of the right things. Okay, she did see some early warning signs. For instance, he started breaking dates because he had to work late. He still wanted to spend a lot of time with the fellas instead of spending nice, romantic evenings with her. Saying, "I love you," became less and less frequent. But those things didn't matter back then. She honestly believed Daniel was her refuge from a lifetime of loneliness.

As she emptied the rest of the wine from the bottle, she realized what she thought was love was nothing more than an obsession to be someone's wife. And what she didn't count on was not living happily ever after.

So many times we think we know what's best for us and only go to God in prayer for affirmation. Then when things don't go as we have planned, we question, "Why did you let this happen, God?"

APPLICATION

The Bible doesn't look favorably upon divorce. As a matter of fact, the Word discourages it. Unfortunately, we live in a society that is more secular than spiritual—making the dissolution of a marriage almost as easy as buying your favorite CD.

If God blesses you with a mate, it's not his will to see it fail. He wants you to succeed! He has as much a stake in your marriage as you do (Mark 10:6-9). But you know what happens, ladies? Some of us tend to forget the prayers we prayed and what we were really praying for. Once we've got him "hooked," we start believing it was our looks or personality or...(hello!) our sexuality that won him over. What we neglect to do is keep on praying (1 Thessalonians 5:17,18).

God gave his Word that he would never leave us or forsake us. If you continue to pray without ceasing you will be blessed. That's God's promise to you, and you know his Word is as good as gold! If you are thinking about getting a divorce, kneel down right now and bring everything to God in prayer. Tell him your whole story—especially what you may have done wrong. And then wait for his answers to start coming.

When you pray, it's important to remember to put God's agenda first instead of your own desires. Learn to submit completely and seek direction and guidance through the Word (Psalm 119:105-106).

PRAYER

Heavenly Father, thank you for being the light of my life and the joy of my salvation. Thank you for loving me. I pray that you'll guide me as I face the trials and tribulations of my marriage. My heart is heavy, Lord, but I know you are the source of my strength and the strength of my life. Thank you for your grace and mercy that follows me even when I don't deserve it. In Jesus' name I pray, Amen.

DAY 2

Weathering the Storm

AFTER THE DIVORCE...

*"Let all bitterness, and wrath, and anger,
and clamour, and evil speaking,
be put away from you, with all malice."*

EPHESIANS 4:31

Depression, anger, frustration, loneliness, confusion. Those are some of the emotions Tasha felt after she walked away from what was supposed to be a lifetime commitment. Seventeen years of her life—gone with the stroke of a pen. Her divorce was final. And now as far as she's concerned, her hopes, dreams, and life s she knew it ended with the marriage.

The problems in the marriage could've been worked out if only he had been more attentive, more loving, more patient, more responsible, and more understanding of her needs. He had taken away the joy of what was once a vibrant, passionate, and assertive woman.

The scars from divorce are not only painful, but they can also take a long time to heal. How could something that seemed so right in the beginning turn out to be so wrong in the end? It's a question that aches throughout every part of our body (Jeremiah 15:18).

APPLICATION

The feelings of loneliness and despair, along with a broken heart, may seem too much to bear. You may feel as if you're losing your mind. But just when your spirit is weakest, that's when God is at his best (Psalm 73:26). Even when you give up on God, he never gives up on you. He is always there waiting for your call, prepared to listen, and eager to pour out a blessing (Matthew 11:28-30).

When we face the storms in our lives, like separation and divorce, we tend to lose sight of our faith. But it's times like these when we need God more than ever—not just once in a while, but every day, every hour, every minute. Won't you try him today?

PRAYER

Father God, thank you for the breath of life that allows me to call on you. Everyday I know I fall short, but I'm so grateful for the grace and mercy that follows me all the days of my life. I know I can't make it on my own. I need you, Lord. I ask you to help me weather this storm so I can see the new light of a new day in your presence. In your son Jesus' name, Amen.

DAY 3

There's Healing for Your Soul

THE FRIENDS WHO STICK BY...

*"Peace I leave with you, my peace I give unto you:
not as the world giveth, give I unto you.
Let not your heart be troubled,
neither let it be afraid."*

JOHN 14:27

After months of what seemed like dead-end therapy, Charlene decided it was time to come out of her cocoon. Her girlfriend, Marva, called and invited her to go on a shopping spree—something they used to do on a weekly basis back in the day. Charlene said she'd go although she wasn't sure if she was ready to deal with the public. But why not? She had been divorced for

almost six months now and everyone kept telling her it was time to rejoin the human race.

Getting together was just like old times—the girls hanging out and spending money like it grew on trees in their backyard. But then at lunch the conversation took on a more serious tone.

Marva said, "Girl, I've been worried about you. You weren't returning my calls, and I think you've forgotten what the inside of a church looks like."

Charlene, feeling uncomfortable and defensive, fired back, "I can handle my business. No need to worry about sista, girl! And as far as church goes, I just haven't been feeling it."

"That's obviously your problem," Marva replied, "you've been trying to handle everything on your own. You need to let go and let God."

That evening when Charlene returned home, she sat in what used to be her ex's favorite chair. She stared at the Bible on the coffee table for a moment and then went to her favorite Scripture, Psalm 121. After reading it several times, she got down on her knees and prayed. When she finished, she called Marva and simply said, "Thank you!"

APPLICATION

God places people in our lives for a reason. Through them he can spread his message of faith, hope, healing, and love. Friends offer support and encouragement when we can't seem to get a grip on the turmoil facing us (Proverbs 18:24). There is also a great source of comfort in the Word (Psalm 119:50). When you put the two together, you have an unbeatable combination!

Who is there in your life that has been helping you through this time of divorce? Thank God right now for that person and consider sending a note or an email thanking that person for her influence on your life.

PRAYER

Dear Lord, I thank you, first of all, for giving me the strength to see another day. This is a day that you have made. I thank you for the friends you have placed in my life. Through them and through your Word, I am finding a healing place. I ask that you continue to strengthen my spirit so that I may serve thee better. In Jesus' name I pray, Amen.

DAY 4

The Breaking of Day

SOMETIMES IT TAKES MORE...

"Restore unto me the joy of thy salvation;
and uphold me with thy free spirit.
Then will I teach transgressors thy ways;
and sinners shall be converted unto thee."

PSALM 51:12-13

While sitting in church one Sunday, Elizabeth felt a strange sensation come over her as the choir sang one of her favorite hymns, "We Exalt Thee." Tears started streaming down her face. They were uncontrollable. The harder she tried to keep them from falling, the faster they fell. She excused herself from her seat and stepped into the corridor to regain her composure. Elizabeth was not one to show emotion in church or anywhere else, for that matter. Sure, she would clap her hands with the choir and nod her head in agreement with the pastor. But she was not a shouter or a crier. That just wasn't in her nature.

But today seemed to be out of her control. It was if she had stepped outside of herself and was observing someone she didn't know. Pastor started preaching from the book of Job. The only thing she remembered hearing him talk about was the drama in Job's life and how his patience and endurance led to an abundance of blessings from God. At that point, Elizabeth knew she had received her breakthrough.

Remember the last time it rained for days and days? You kept thinking, "I'll be glad when the sun finally comes shining through." Then the clouds started to give way to bright, glorious sunshine. It changed your mood from gloomy to happy.

That's the same thing God does for your spirit. He will revive you from a broken marriage. Right before your eyes (and the eyes of those around you), God will change your appearance and your focus (2 Corinthians 4:17). He will give you a new attitude and a sense of peace and tranquility. Are you ready for your breakthrough? Then claim it today!

APPLICATION

Sometimes you are too depressed. Look back on the last week. How many days have you felt "under the weather"? How many days has your mood been negative? If it was most days, and if that has been going on for weeks, consider getting help. You especially need to see someone if you are not sleeping or if your weight is going up or down dramatically.

Claim God's promises today. Look for a breakthrough. If it doesn't come, then consider seeking help from a pastor or Christian counselor. Sometimes it takes more than a hymn to break through the sadness.

PRAYER

Dear Lord, I know you are the source of my strength and I thank you for your everlasting love and peace. Thank you for opening my eyes and allowing me to see that I can always find comfort in you. I ask that you continue to guide me as I face whatever new battles come my way. Lord, you are worthy to be praised. All these blessings I ask in your wonderful son Jesus' name, Amen.

HOW I GOT OVER!!!

*"Therefore if any man be in Christ,
he is a new creature: old things are passed away;
behold, all things are become new."*

2 CORINTHIANS 5:17

My soul looks back and wonders, how I got over..." Aja didn't know all the words to the spiritual she used to hear her grandmother sing when she was a child. But that didn't matter. Her heart was filled with joy. and those were the words that filled her soul. Today marked the one-year anniversary of her divorce. For a moment she reflected. She thought of all the tears, the lonely and sleepless nights, the hurt, anger, and guilt. She recalled how she cursed her ex over and

over again, and how she made the children feel that the marital problems were their fault.

But that was history. Right now, she had a sense of calm and direction. She had purpose and determination. Her happiness was genuine. Life was good because God was good. He took a broken down, battered woman and made her whole again.

As Aja walked over to the mirror in her bathroom, she stared in amazement. She strutted her stuff, proud as a peacock, and commenced to singing, "My soul looks back and wonders, how I got over..."

APPLICATION

Renewing your spirit after a divorce can be a long and painful journey. But the good news is you don't have to travel alone on that road to recovery. Jesus is standing patiently, ready to heal your wounds (Matthew 7:7,8).

You have to learn to stop blaming others for your shortcomings and let God deal with the one who hurt you. Stop living in the past and focus on your future. Stop complaining about the fact that he doesn't pay child support or the fact that he hardly sees his children. God has put you in charge of your life and your household. He will supply your needs. Trust him.

PRAYER

Heavenly Father, I come before you today thanking you for peace of mind. You've healed my broken spirit. I ask that you forgive me for my sins and forgive me for the way I've treated my ex-husband. One day you will bring me to a place in my heart where I can forgive my ex. I ask that you continue to watch over my family and strengthen our bond. And thank you for your son Jesus in whose name I pray, Amen.

JUNE
WEEK FOUR: COVENANT

DAY 1
First things first

WHAT IS A COVENANT?

*"And be not conformed to this world:
but be ye transformed by the renewing of your mind,
that ye may prove what is that good, and acceptable,
and perfect, will of God."*

ROMANS 12:2

One word that has a clear and concise meaning is in the Bible is "covenant." A covenant is an everlasting vow. In the Christian community, a covenant is an agreement made before God. Unlike a contract that has terms and loopholes, a covenant is an agreement to be kept; it does not change with circumstances—the terms are set from the beginning.

Marriage is a covenant. With the divorce rate hovering around 60 percent for Christians and non-Christians alike, it is safe to say that many people do not consult the bible or a dictionary before getting married. Marriage is a covenant with the terms "till death do us part." The words spoken at a marriage celebration are called vows. Numbers 30:2 defines a vow as, "If a man vow a vow unto the Lord, or swear an oath to bind his soul with a bond; he shall not break his word." God speaks plainly in that verse.

APPLICATION

If you are considering marriage, you must enter the covenant with the mindset that this is your first and only marriage. If you are married, you must have the mindset that this is it until death do you part.

PRAYER

Heavenly Father, we thank you for giving us the opportunity to show love the way you love us, unconditionally. Help us to remember that our worldly marriages are to be an imitation of the marriage between the church and you. In Jesus name, Amen.

DAY 2

No Excuses

"DON'T QUIT"

"Charity never faileth: but whether there be prophecies, they shall fail; whether there be tongues, they shall cease; whether there be knowledge, it shall vanish away."

1 CORINTHIANS 13:8

I have been married for twelve years. Occasionally, a young person will ask my advice on marriage. This always makes me laugh because my marriage has been an adventure. No matter what the question is about, my advice is pretty consistent: Don't quit. My advice, albeit simplistic, is good advice because God gives me the same advice every day of my marriage.

Marriage is no cake walk. Marriage takes hard work, patience and tenacity. No matter how discouraged you may become, tomorrow is a new day. As a Christians we are instructed to renew our minds (Romans 12:1,2).

After the honeymoon is over, remember to encourage yourselves. It is a cliché, but it is also true that it is always darkest before the dawn.

APPLICATION

You are probably familiar with 1 Corinthians 13, the love chapter. The eighth verse says, "Charity never faileth." Other translations say, "love never quits." It's been said that there is no greater love than a mother's love. Well, God's love is even greater. His love is unconditional. The Bible is full of encouragement and promises. It is really simple. God gives us a lifetime to work on ourselves and our relationships.

Read 1 Corinthians 13:4-8 out loud and personalize it by inserting your name and the name of your spouse.

PRAYER

Dear Lord, Thank you for being an example for us. Help us to love our mates the way you love us—unconditionally. Amen.

DAY 3

God's Covenant Example

DO AS I DO...

Idon't know how many times my sons catch me breaking my own rules. It is so humbling for me when I tell them not to do something like drink soda for breakfast and they say, "But you do, mom." I am so thankful that God follows his own rules. God is a covenant God. God would not ask us to do something he would not do first.

When God makes a covenant, it is everlasting. The Bible provides us with many covenant examples in the Bible, such as his covenant with Abraham (Gen. 17:10-11), Moses (Ex. 24:3-8), and Noah (Gen 9:8-10). The conditions for the covenants are the same, irrevocable. God is our example. He follows his rules. We never see him doing something that we cannot do.

APPLICATION

Christian families should strive to live in a way that demonstrates dedication to family and covenant and that offers an example to our children in an effort to do what God says do.

Use a concordance to look up passages on covenant. Write up a list of words that define God's covenants. Do these apply to your family?

PRAYER

Dear Lord, help us to remember that people pay more attention to our lives than our words. Thank you that your Word is our example. Amen.

DAY 4

Look in the Mirror

FIX YOURSELF...

"Nevertheless let every one of you in particular so love his wife even as himself; and the wife see that she reverence her husband."

EPHESIANS 5:33

I like to shop. My favorite stores have what I consider good customer service. Good customer service means getting what I want at a good price. I don't help the salespeople. I expect them to help me. I want things my way.

Some of us enter marriage focusing on what the other person can do for us. But when you enter into a covenant, you make vows. You have terms to fulfill. The other party's actions do not dictate your behavior. God speaks to husbands and wives individually. God speaks directly to each partner about how to treat the other. Good customer service is focused on meeting someone else's needs, just as a good marriage should focus on meeting each other's needs.

APPLICATION

The next time you are out shopping, people in the customer service-both good and bad service. Take note of the differences and how you can work to improve your attitude and service to your mate and family at home.

PRAYER

Lord, forgive us for our selfishness. Give us a servant's heart. Show us the joy of serving. Amen.

DAY 5

It is Worth It

HAVE
FAITH...

*"Now faith is the substance of things hoped for,
the evidence of things not seen."*

HEBREWS 11:1

Volunteers are a special breed of people. They perform jobs and tasks without monetary compensation. Volunteers reap intangible benefits. It is highly unlikely that most people would answer a want ad that read, "Work for 40 hours a week, 50 weeks a year, just for the fun of it." A paycheck is a reward for executing tasks and responsibilities. Your paycheck should not be your sole motivation for working, but it is a reward for a completed job. Employees have faith that they will receive compensation on a designated date. On a typical payday, employees confidently collect their pay.

Christians should approach their marriage with the same confident expectation. Hebrews 10:35,36 says, "Cast not away your confidence which hath great recompense of reward... that, after ye have done the will of God, ye might receive the promise." If your marriage is not where you want it to be, have faith, have hope.

Most of us enter marriage looking at the existing attributes of our mate. Over time, as people change their attributes and characteristics change. It may become difficult for a marriage to survive this change unless both parties are willing to grow and work together.

APPLICATION

How many couples have faith that their future is going to be better than their pasts? Faith is an essential part of covenant. Faith keeps you committed when you do not like your mate and when your mate does not like you. It will get better. Have faith!

You may not have any tangible benefits in your relationships right now, but remember that you always have faith. Faith can get you through when nothing else will. Have faith in your Heavenly Father—he has never lost hope in us.

PRAYER

Dear God, help us to see things through your eyes. You see us with eyes of faith. Thank you for faith. Amen.

JULY
WEEK ONE: WORRY

DAY 1

The Wonder of Worry

BLOOM WHERE YOU'RE PLANTED...

"Not that I speak in respect of want: for I have learned, in whatsoever state I am, therewith to be content. I know both how to be abased, and I know how to abound: everywhere and in all things I am instructed both to be full and to be hungry, both to abound and to suffer need."

PHILIPPIANS 4:11-12

Several years ago, Brittany was required to move to a small town for her job. From the instant she set foot in the town, she disliked it. The people moved at a slow pace. There was no movie theatre or shopping mall nearby, so there was nothing to do in her spare time. The job was uninteresting. She needed to find a way to relocate; otherwise, she was afraid she might get stuck—overlooked by headquarters.

Two years went by, and she was still there because she had no job offers. She worried every day about when she would leave. But God had a big lesson for her. God began teaching Brittany the secret of contentment, and after a while she began to notice that a different attitude was taking hold. One day, she came home from work, looked around and realized that her apartment was really nice. On another occasion, she found herself thanking some coworkers for their help with a project. And she started a couple of hobbies she'd been meaning to learn but had been too busy to get into before. Later, when she finally received a job offer in a major city, she turned it down.

APPLICATION

Many times, we worry so much about our present situation that we forget to appreciate our current circumstances. We receive many blessings on a daily basis, but many of us fail to recognize them. Today, take a few minutes to reflect on gratitude and contentment. Write down five things for which you are grateful or that you are content with just as things exist right now.

PRAYER

Lord, thank You for all of Your many blessings and for showing me the people, places, and things around me right here and now that You have put in place. There is no need for me to worry. Help me to keep my focus on You and all the good things in my life. Amen.

DAY 2

Living for Today

THE SIDE EFFECTS OF WORRY...

"Take therefore no thought for the morrow:
for the morrow shall take thought
for the things of itself.
Sufficient unto the day is the evil thereof."
MATTHEW 6:34

At 25, Maria Smith was told she had an ulcer. Although Maria was upset about the diagnosis, she was not completely surprised. She had a stressful job as an engineer, she had recently married and moved to a new city, and she had just learned that a baby was on the way.

Just a few days later, Maria's husband told her that a competitor bought his company and layoffs were inevitable. Despite this, Maria knew she needed a calm frame of mind—especially for the baby's sake. She needed the assurance of faith. It was time to acknowledge that God is in control. To help her relax, she began writing down her worries and sharing them with God. As her worries diminished, her ulcer got better and her prenatal health was good, too.

APPLICATION

God loves us and wants us to let Him help us live and learn. Create a God box. The box can be as simple or as elaborate as you like. Gather several slips of paper, and on each one write down one worry you are experiencing. Then place it in the box and ask for God's help in how best to handle the situation and learn from it. Write down as many worries as you like. The God box reminds you to cast your cares on Him—and then rest assured that He will help you.

PRAYER

Lord, today I cast my cares on You, knowing that You will show me how I should resolve difficulties. You know best how I should handle problems. I know that You care about me, and I am thankful for Your faith and love. Amen.

DAY 3

Listening to God

WAITING TO EXHALE...

"So I spake unto you; and ye would not hear,
but rebelled against the commandment of the Lord,
and went presumptuously up into the hill."

DEUTERONOMY 1:43

Remember when Terry McMillan's book Waiting to Exhale was popular? Women of color everywhere—at the beauty shop, on the subway, in the doctor's office—had their noses buried in that book. In a way, McMillan's novel was allowing its readers to "exhale." For a few minutes each day, personal troubles were set aside, overtaken by interest in what was happening in the lives of fictional characters. While it's important not to let entertainment become an excuse for avoiding everyday reality altogether, letting go of our worries is something we should do on a daily basis.

APPLICATION

We are told to take our burdens to the Lord, and we need to wait on God and listen to what He is saying to us. God speaks to us all the time. Are we listening? Take a few minutes of quiet, private time every morning or evening. Enjoy a cup of herbal tea, jot a few thoughts to God, and then be still and listen to Him. You might even plan a monthly retreat where you do something totally focused on God for a day or two. Try a retreat center or book a room at a secluded inn, away from daily distractions. It's amazing how "getting away from it all" puts your worries into perspective.

PRAYER

Lord, I thank You for this day. Please help me to keep You at the forefront of my thoughts and actions. Help me to relax, be quiet, and get in touch with Your gracious Spirit within me. Help me to see that You are at work, opening doors on my behalf. Amen.

DAY 4

The Secret of My Success

ASK FOR HELP...

*"And let them judge the people at all seasons:
and it shall be, that every great matter they shall bring
unto thee, but every small matter they shall judge:
so shall it be easier for thyself, and they shall bear the
burden with thee. If thou shalt do this thing, and God
command thee so, then thou shalt be able to endure,
and all this people shall also go to their place in peace."*

EXODUS 18:22–23

What is the secret of your success?" a member of the audience asked a well-known speaker after a prayer breakfast at a local church.

"God has taught me how to delegate," she replied. She explained that, like many other people, she went through times when she was too busy to take care of every responsibility on her own. She delegated some of her duties to others; and even though people didn't always handle things as well she would have done if she'd had the time to do them herself, she learned to adjust her expectations. She learned to stop worrying about mishaps and let people do things as best they could.

The speaker said, "God helped me understand that I'm a better businesswoman because of this; but, more importantly, I am a better servant of God."

APPLICATION

We are all tempted to believe that we are superhuman, but we are not and neither are the people to whom we delegate some responsibilities. And in delegating to friends, relatives, and others, we also must learn to let go. If your daughter does her own laundry, don't expect the clothes to look just as they would if you did it. If a coworker takes longer on a report than you would have taken, encouraging the person's efforts eases your workplace relationship and helps the person feel valued at their job. Make a list of at least five tasks you need to accomplish. Instead of worrying how you will get them done, delegate them. Remember to praise people's efforts so that they are glad they assisted you.

PRAYER

Lord, thank You for surrounding me with people who can help me accomplish the things I need to get done. Help me to hand my burdens over, be at peace with my decisions, and praise those who help me. Amen.

DAY 5

Letting Go and Letting God

GET OUT OF YOUR OWN WAY...

"Hear me, O Lord; for thy lovingkindness is good: turn unto me according to the multitude of thy tender mercies."

PSALM 69:16

Marla was turning 30 and she still wasn't married. She prayed and prayed, but nothing happened. Then Marla began dating a man who had some decent qualities, but he drank too much and didn't attend church regularly. Marla told her best friend Paul that she was tired of God taking His time; she was ready to get married. Paul told her that no matter what she decided he would still be her friend and pray for her happiness.

Marla convinced the man to marry her and began making wedding plans. But then she told Paul that she didn't feel as happy as she thought she would. She realized her feelings for Paul were deeper and stronger than her feelings for her fiancé. When she called off the wedding, the man didn't seem bothered at all. On the other hand, Paul let her know that he meant what he said about remaining her steady, best friend. After a while, Paul told her that after they planned their future the right way—together, with God's help—he would buy her an engagement ring and they would get married. Marla realized that she had been so busy worrying about being married that she hadn't noticed the one man who was always there for her. Her "Mr. Right" was Paul, who had been by her side all along.

APPLICATION

Oftentimes, we say that we've given a worrisome situation to the Lord; but if we look closely enough, we can spot our fingerprints all over the circumstances. We think we are helping, but God does not need our help. If we truly believe in Him, we will get out of the way, put the situation into His hands, and have peace in knowing that everything is going to be all right. Take a situation in your life—big or small—that is bothering you and vow to let it go. This will be easier said than done. If something is troubling you so much that you have restless sleep, can't stop talking about it, can't focus on your work or family responsibilities, or have become physically sick (with headaches, for example) take it to the Lord and leave it there.

PRAYER

Lord, today I give my dreams and my burdens to You. I know that You want me to let go of the negative situations and let You do Your work in my life. Help me to trust You to deliver me from my burdens. Amen.

JULY
WEEK TWO: ADULTERY

DAY 1

Opening the Cage Door

LOVING AN UNBELIEVER...

"If any brother hath a wife that believeth not,
and she be pleased to dwell with him,
let him not put her away. And the woman which hath
an husband that believeth not, and if he be pleased
to dwell with her, let her not leave him.
But if the unbelieving depart, let him depart.
A brother or a sister is not under bondage in such cases:
but God hath called us to peace."

1 CORINTHIANS 7:12B-13, 15

Winston and Olivia had been married for seven years. Olivia was a faithful believer, but Winston had abandoned his faith shortly after they were married. The past year had been extremely difficult for them. Winston's behavior

had changed from warm and loving to cold and distant. Olivia prayed for Winston and their marriage every day. The things she did that normally would have pleased him—keeping the house clean, cooking his favorite meals, wearing outfits that he used to compliment, coming straight home from her job—did nothing to change his attitude toward her. Lately, he was staying out more and more, and returning home later and later.

One Friday evening, Winston came home and announced that he was leaving. He told Olivia that he had found another woman, with whom he had been having an affair. He said that he was tired of hiding and feeling guilty. He had to do what he felt was best for him.

APPLICATION

Get a beautiful gift box that is large enough to hold several index cards. Make a list of things that you feel are problem areas in a relationship or marriage that you are in currently or that has recently ended. Ask God to give you guidance about what you should do concerning each problem. If your husband has already moved out, ask God to give you a spirit of reconciliation and a spirit of peace. Write your prayers on the index cards and put them in the box. Include prayers for your loved one, yourself, and your relationship. Add more prayer requests as God leads you. At the end of every three months, take the prayer requests out of your box and see how God has answered them.

PRAYER

Lord Jesus, as it is written in John 14:27, You said, "My peace I give you." I ask for Your comfort and peace today. Thank You for Your love and for giving us the choice to love You of our own free will. Help us to love those who have hurt us. Help us to give them the freedom to love us back. Amen.

DAY 2

Facing Temptation

RESIST THE DEVIL AND HE WILL FLEE...

*"Then was Jesus led up of the Spirit into the wilderness
to be tempted by the devil. Then saith Jesus unto him,
Get thee hence, Satan; for it is written,
Thou shalt worship the Lord thy God,
and him only shall thou serve."*

MATTHEW 4:1, 10

Estella was happy to be going out of town to attend a conference for small business owners. Her business was doing pretty well—much better than her marriage. She suspected that her husband was having an affair, and she was tired of trying to figure out how to make things right between them. She was contemplating a separation. Estella felt that God had turned a deaf ear to her prayers.

On the last night of the conference, Estella was finishing her dessert when a gentleman who also had been attending the conference sat down at her table. They laughed and talked for hours, trading stories about the ups and downs of their businesses. But when he invited her to spend more time with him in either of their hotel rooms, Estella was jolted back to reality. She told him that she was married and the evening was over. She left him at the table and returned to her hotel room. That night, the Bible in her room helped her as she reached new clarity about her marriage.

APPLICATION

What will you do when you've been wronged and the awful thought sneaks in that even God seems to have abandoned you? This path leads to Satan and destruction. The path that brings you through every challenge and strengthens you also brings you closer to God. Jesus faced temptation, betrayal, gossip, lies, and crucifixion. God brought Him through each situation. Use Him as your model. God has promised to provide a way out for you.

Jesus used the Scriptures to chase Satan away. Write down your greatest temptation and find Scriptures to help you to overcome it. Memorize these Scriptures, and when the temptation arises, declare the appropriate verses to yourself. This will reinforce what you have determined within your spirit. Continue to do this until you have the victory.

PRAYER

Lord God, You are my Shepherd. Your rod and staff comfort me. Walk with me as I go through valleys that include wrongful behavior. Deliver me from evil so that I do not yield to temptation. Restore my joy so that I do not sin against You. Amen.

DAY 3
Father, Take This Cup

HOW WOULD YOU RESPOND?

*"Father, if thou be willing, remove this cup from me:
nevertheless, not my will, but thine, be done."*

LUKE 22:42

Nearly every week Brian—a tall, handsome man in his sixties—waited for his wife to go to church, called his lover, and invited her over to the house. As God would have it, one day Brian's wife came home early from church. There Brian was, in bed with another woman. After the woman left, Brian went to the kitchen where his wife was preparing Sunday dinner as usual. He wondered how she could behave as though nothing was wrong. He packed a suitcase, anticipating that leaving was the next step. But

when he went to see what his wife would say, she told him that dinner was ready. They ate as if nothing had happened.

Brian never moved out, and she didn't ask him to. But as time went by, his conscience bothered him more and more. He stopped his adultery, but this did not end his inner struggle. One night while his wife was at church, he began to cry. He got on his knees and asked for God's forgiveness. He asked Jesus to come into his heart. After that, a sense of peace came over him.

His wife never mentioned the Sunday when she came home early from church. But Brian starts each day by getting down on his knees to thank God for sending His Son Jesus who took away his sins and for giving him his wife.

APPLICATION

On the night before His death, Jesus went to the Garden of Gethsemane to plead with His Father to come up with another plan. But God did not provide plan B. Jesus said, "Nevertheless, not my will but thy will be done" (Luke 22:42). Whatever your pain and suffering is, it will come to an end. How it ends up depends on the choices you make and your faith in God.

Think of a betrayal in your life. Pray and ask God how you can show love to the person involved. If someone has betrayed you, write a letter to let the person know that you have forgiven him or her. If you have wronged someone, tell that person that you want to ask for his or her forgiveness.

᠅

PRAYER

Thank You for sending Your Son Jesus to save me from my sins. Help me to remain faithful to You in the face of pain and suffering. Give me the power to love those who have betrayed me and resist the sin of betraying others. Show me how I can "be Jesus" to them. Amen.

DAY 4

He Wasn't My Husband

IS IT YOU OR YOUR HUSBAND?

*"Jesus said unto her, Thou hast well said,
I have no husband: For thou hast had five husbands;
and he who thou now hast is not thy husband:
in that saidest thou truly."*

JOHN 4:17B-18

Darla saw how her brothers treated women. Because she wanted to be like them, she was the female version of a "player." Her parents sent her to live with her aunt in the South, hoping to slow her down. It didn't happen.

She married an older guy who was friends with her aunt. She ended up marrying him not for love, but for the things he could give her. He was hardworking, loving, faithful, and good to her, but she had married him for the things he could give her. She grew bored with him, and one day she met a married man who made her feel special; she thought. The fact that both of them were married did not matter.

Darla got a job so she could get her own apartment, and she left her husband. Eventually, the other man separated from his wife and moved in with her. After about a year or so, they had a son. She wanted to get married and live as a family. But instead of marrying Darla, the man went back to his wife.

APPLICATION

One day, when Jesus was sitting by a well, a Samaritan woman came by; and Jesus did something unusual for that time: He spoke to the woman, a Samaritan. Jesus told her the truth about her lifestyle. As they continued to talk, Jesus told her that He is the Messiah. She realized her thirst for His truth, and she returned to town to tell others about Jesus. When the people heard, they believed in Him. Allow God to speak to your heart today.

Make a list of people in your family tree. Look to see if there are patterns of adultery, immorality, divorce, and so on. Pray for those family members who are still living. Ask God to restore the relationships wherever possible. If you are in a sinful relationship, ask the Holy Spirit to help you. Then tell others what God has done for you so that they will want to know Jesus as Savior. Ask God to use you to break the cycle of broken relationships.

PRAYER

O God, surely there is no greater love than that shown by the One who lay down His life for my sins. Forgive me and the members of my family for our sin-filled relationships. Give me the desire to become intimate with You as I let You show me how to replace adultery and other misbehavior with faithfulness, kindness, and love. Help me to get to know You better and to use my body to bring honor and glory to You. Amen.

DAY 5

I Know What You Are Doing

BE NOT DECEIVED...

*"But the fearful, and unbelieving,
and the abominable, and murderers, and whoremongers,
and sorcerers, and idolaters, and all liars,
shall have their part in the lake which
burneth with fire...."*

REVELATION 21:8

Reverends Marshall and Lydia Nelson were co-pastors of their growing church. They had been married for 14 years and had two children. Although their ministry was flourishing, their marriage was not.

Lydia decided to get her master's degree, and she joined a study group. She especially

liked Bruce, one of the group members, and they began meeting for lunch by themselves. Marshall noticed changes in Lydia's behavior. She got a new hairstyle and a lot of new outfits. After Marshall surprised her one day by turning up at the seminary during lunchtime, he saw Bruce and Lydia together and sensed an attraction between them. That evening, Lydia confessed that her relationship with Bruce, although platonic, was more than friendship. They decided to undergo counseling, and Lydia agreed to stop spending time with Bruce.

But Lydia still felt unfulfilled. She began having lunch with a fellow board member of a local charity organization. She even went to a hotel with him, but then she changed her mind and left. She felt she was no longer fit to be a wife or a minister, and she entered individual counseling. She told her counselor that she could not blame Marshall for their troubles. The sin was in her heart.

APPLICATION

Emotional entanglement, pornography, and sex talk in a chat room are as destructive to the marital relationship as infidelity and intercourse. They are just as difficult to overcome because of the hold they have on the mind. If Lydia's story is your story, take a serious look at what you are doing and the price you will have to pay. Is the relationship with this other person worth destroying your marriage, your family, your self-respect, and your eternal relationship with God? All are at stake. You can't fool God. He knows what you are doing.

The Prayer of Jabez is a simple, powerful prayer taken from 1 Chronicles 4:10: "And Jabez called on the God of Israel, saying, Oh that thou wouldest bless me indeed, and enlarge my coast, and that thine hand might be with me, and that thou wouldest keep me from evil, that it may not grieve me!" Write this prayer on index cards and post it in prominent places where you can see it throughout the day. Pray especially that God's hand will be on you. When you ask for His help, He will keep you from evil.

PRAYER

Lord God, have mercy on us. Deliver us from the spirit of adultery, lust, and immorality. Surround us with Your protective hedge, so that we might not sin against You. We thank You that You take us back and forgive us when we fall short of Your glory. Help us to live lives that will be pleasing to You. Help us to be faithful to You, O Lord. Amen.

JULY
WEEK THREE: REVENGE

DAY 1
Weigh Your Options

THE SUFFERING CAN'T COMPARE...

"For I reckon that the sufferings of this present time are not worthy to be compared with the glory which shall be revealed in us."
ROMANS 8:18

Natalie and Sheila were best friends. Natalie was plain, not confrontational, and had a boyfriend named Eddie. Sheila thought of herself as beautiful, was a flirt, and had no boyfriend. One Saturday, they were going shopping for swimsuits to wear to a neighborhood pool party. When Natalie arrived at Sheila's house,

Sheila's sister let her in and Natalie headed straight upstairs to Sheila's bedroom. Natalie overheard a phone conversation that Sheila was having.

"No matter what swimsuit Natalie buys," Sheila said, "you know I will look better. Eddie thinks I'm finer than Natalie. When he sees me in my swimsuit, I think I'm gonna take him from that girl. You know that's right."

Sheila's sister tried to pull Natalie away and get her to go back downstairs. But Natalie barely heard her. She was wounded to the quick. How could her best friend say things like that about her—and how could she make such comments about her boyfriend? Feelings of betrayal began to overtake Natalie. She had a mind to march right into Sheila's bedroom and confront her.

APPLICATION

When we are deeply hurt, our natural instinct is to strike back. The Bible says that our sufferings can't compare to the glory that will be revealed in us; so when we weigh our options, we will see that it is better to wait for the glory than to take matters into our own hands.

Practice pressing your "pause" button. Stand in front of the mirror and imagine a close friend has just betrayed you. Look at yourself and think about your reaction. Then imagine pressing a button within you that enables you to pause, stop your angry thoughts, and take control of your emotions. Choose not to perpetuate the wrong by seeking revenge. Role-playing can be a powerful tool in developing a skill like self-control. Pray for the Holy Spirit to calm your emotions, help you gather your thoughts, and then direct you on a constructive next step.

PRAYER

Father God, I get very upset when wrong is done to me. Please help me find my pause button. I want You to be pleased with me, Lord. Let me feel Your presence in and around me so that the negative feelings I experience are swallowed up in Your love. Thank You, Jesus. Amen.

DAY 2

Plant Good Seed

SEED TIME AND HARVEST...

"While the earth remaineth, seedtime and harvest, and cold and heat, and summer and winter, and day and night shall not cease."

GENESIS 8:22

Joann knew that she had put a fifty-dollar bill in the jewelry box on her dresser. It was there when she left for work but was gone when she got home. The only person who had been there was Martha, the cleaning lady. But Martha had worked for Joann for two years now and had never stolen anything. Joann had always been very pleased with Martha's work. But she could think of no other explanation. No one else had a key to her condo. She didn't want to hurt

Martha's feelings by accusing her of stealing, but she had to know.

When Joann confronted Martha, her guilty look confirmed Joann's suspicions; but Martha denied stealing the money. Joann remembered conversations the women had about Martha's son. She sensed that Martha was having problems with her son again. Joann didn't want to fire Martha—but she couldn't have a thief cleaning her home. She pressed Martha to open up. Finally, Martha broke down and confessed. She explained to Joann that she needed money to bail her son out of jail. Joann now had a decision to make.

APPLICATION

If we stopped to consider the consequences of our actions more often, we would do more good than harm. Genesis 8 tells us that as long as the earth remains, there will be seedtime and harvest. Whatever we sow, we will reap. Being kind to a wrongdoer may help in the healing process. Love and forgiveness are powerful tools that can often lead to a change of attitude and positive behavior. If you sow a "do good" seed by blessing those who curse you, the good seed will return a good harvest to you. If someone is out to harm you, he or she will reap what they sow.

When someone has hurt or wronged you, bless them by sowing a "do good" seed. Was the infraction intentional? Are there any extenuating circumstances (such as the fact that Martha's son was in jail in the case above)? Once you know the truth, take the high road and be an example of forgiveness. Give the offender an opportunity to correct the wrong. Be prepared to forgive as God has always forgiven you.

PRAYER

Lord, You said to bless them that curse me. I bless my enemies in the name of Jesus. I pray that truth and wisdom be revealed to them, and that they may be driven to repentance. As I forgive them, I thank You for forgiving me. Thank You for the harvest, the victory, the peace, love, and joy in the midst of this situation. Amen.

DAY 3

God's Got This

VENGEANCE IS MINE...

"Dearly beloved, avenge not yourselves,
but rather give place unto wrath: for it is written,
Vengeance is mine; I will repay, saith the Lord."

ROMANS 12:19

Stephanie wasn't in the habit of loaning out her car and was reluctant to do so when her neighbor Rachel said she was in an emergency and asked to borrow it. Stephanie's instincts were right. Rachel hit a deer, causing significant damage to Stephanie's car. Stephanie decided not to report the accident to her insurance provider. Instead, she insisted that Rachel pay for the repairs, which Rachel said she would do when she had the money. But Rachel never seemed to have the money. Stephanie paid for the repairs herself, and Rachel continued saying that she couldn't afford it yet.

Months passed and Stephanie noticed that Rachel bought a new car. It was becoming apparent to Stephanie that Rachel had no intention of reimbursing her for the damage she caused to her car. She was irritated and frustrated every time she saw Rachel driving her new car. Stephanie realized she had a choice: She could continue to wait for Rachel to pay her, or she could sue her.

APPLICATION

Forgiving is not forgetting. Of course, you can't erase an event from your brain. Romans 12:19 tells us to "give place unto [God's] wrath"—in other words, don't get mad. Ignore what you can, and pray a hedge of protection around yourself. Stay focused on being who you are instead of focusing on the wrong done to you. You will remain true to yourself, and you will not be overcome by bitterness or resentment.

When someone has wronged you, tell yourself: God's got this. Notice the way you react in the presence of someone who has wronged you because this will tell you if you have forgiven the person. If you notice that anger or frustration arises when the person comes into your presence—keep praying. You have not forgiven him or her. If your attitude remains the same before, during, and after the person's presence then you have forgiven him or her. You are the victor and no longer the victim. You can lead your life free of the shackles of bitterness.

PRAYER

Lord, there are so many injustices to forgive and overlook. There are so many debts that have not been paid. Yet You paid my debt. I could never have paid it myself. So, I can forgive the debt of others and rid myself of the pain they caused. In Jesus' name. Amen!

DAY 4

The Big Payback

WE WRESTLE NOT AGAINST FLESH AND BLOOD...

"For we wrestle not against flesh and blood, but against principalities, against powers, against the rulers of the darkness of this world, against spiritual wickedness in high places."

EPHESIANS 6:12

Karen's husband, Frank was a binge drinker. He got drunk only on weekends, but he was an alcohol abuser nonetheless. During the week, Frank went to work faithfully, came home at night to be with his family, and did chores around the house. He spent his weekends hanging out

with his drinking buddies. Karen knew he had a drinking problem and discussed it with him. But Frank denied it and told her to stop nagging him.

Karen started attending substance abuse meetings at church to learn what she could do to help Frank realize his problem. When she insisted that Frank attend meetings with her, he hit her for the first time. He assured her that he would never hit her again, but he wouldn't agree to go to the meetings with her. She continued to attend though, and the group prayed and stood in agreement with her for her husband's deliverance. And then one evening, Frank walked into a meeting.

APPLICATION

When someone has wronged us, it may not have been intentional. Demonic spirits can cause people to do wrong. Demonic spirits are very real. We are at war with a powerful army whose goal is to defeat Christ's church. When we choose to believe in Christ, Satan's army becomes our adversary, using tricks and people to turn us away from Jesus and back to sin. Even though our victory is assured, we must engage in the struggle until Christ returns. God has equipped us with everything we need to defeat Satan.

Identify three people who have hurt you. Look behind their actions and look for the hand of the devil in their lives. Then pray for their deliverance. Pray for wisdom, strength, understanding, and direction about what God would have you do. Next, bind the enemy according to Matthew 18:18: "Whatsoever ye shall bind on earth shall be bound in heaven."

This includes demonic spirits. Ask the Spirit of God to overtake you or the person who is under attack. Finally, thank God for deliverance.

PRAYER

God, I know that Satan and his demons are often behind the hurtful things that have been done to me. Convict the people who hurt me and make them see how they are allowing themselves to be used by the enemy. I pray for their deliverance from satanic attacks. Give them knowledge of how to obtain and maintain their deliverance. In the name of Jesus, I pray. Amen.

DAY 5
A Good Night's Sleep

WEEPING MAY ENDURE FOR A NIGHT...

"Weeping may endure for a night, but joy cometh in the morning."

PSALM 30:5B

Charlita and Monique were cousins. Charlita was always there for Monique, but as they got older their lives took different turns. Charlita went to college, graduated, got a good job, and bought a home. Monique had a child while she was still a teenager and barely finished high school. Now she had three babies with different daddies and was in love with a married man who had promised her he would leave his wife. Despite their differences, through the years Monique and Charlita stayed in touch. Whenever she was in a bind, Monique called Charlita, who was always there for her.

Charlita even took her cousin and her children into her home for free until Monique could get back on her feet. While Monique and her children were living with her, Charlita was laid off. From her savings, Charlita continued to provide for those in her house.

One day, Monique got into a car accident. She eventually received a large settlement, and her fortunes improved significantly. Some time later, Charlita had an unexpected expense and asked Monique for help. Monique said she couldn't help; she had plans to buy a new car. Charlita was devastated, but she knew that she would soon be back on her feet. She also knew that Monique would probably run out of money soon and again be financially hard up.

APPLICATION

Some of the greatest hurts occur in deep friendships. The pain seems to strike as deeply as the bond in what had seemed to be an unbreakable relationship. When someone has wronged you, leave it to the Lord to work it out. Pray for wisdom about your situation, ask God to reveal to you what it is that He will have you do, and yield to the Holy Spirit's leadership, guidance, and direction as you endure the pain.

Picture one person very close to you who has hurt you deeply. Do you harbor any feelings against that person? Write down why you think you are clinging to those feelings. Then pray to release them and allow yourself to feel better.

PRAYER

God, You know how much those we love can hurt us. Help me to release the hurt feelings from those close relationships. Let me feel the pain and release it to You. Please show me what I need to do and then help me to do it. In Jesus' name. Amen.

JULY
WEEK FOUR: FORGIVENESS

DAY 1
Forgiveness

GOD'S EXTENDED MERCY...

*"If we confess our sins, he is faithful
and just to forgive us
our sins, and to cleanse us from
all unrighteousness."*

1 JOHN 1:9

It was one o'clock in the morning and the air was heavy with the smell of cheap perfume, cigarette smoke, and liquor. A chill in the air caused the woman to pull at the hem of her too-short skirt. As she rounded the corner, she almost walked into him. "Are you looking for a party girl?" she asked.

He paused and spoke slowly. "I would like to have some of your time this evening. Why don't we walk?"

Something about his voice made her agree. They walked for an hour, and she told him about a life that had driven her to the streets. He told her about a man named Jesus who died to pay for all her sins. "You're forgiven," he said. "He paid for the shame, the guilt, and the stain of your sin. You are forgiven."

Believing him, she found in those few words the peace she had long sought for. When she accepted Jesus as Savior, she knew that her life would never be the same.

APPLICATION

Forgiveness is a difficult concept for our minds to grasp. But Christ promises that when we confess our sins, He remembers them no more (see Jeremiah 31:34). For the unbeliever, there is no better news. When we acknowledge our sins and our need of a Savior, He promises to forgive, pardon, and cleanse us of all sin. He died on Calvary's Cross to pay for sin, and we are promised: "There is therefore now no condemnation to them which are in Christ Jesus" (Romans 8:1).

Perhaps in your heart you have felt ashamed of your lifestyle or things in your past. Begin to confess simple, brief prayers to God and open the lines of communication. God hears and answers prayer.

PRAYER

Lord Jesus, I fall before You with outstretched arms. I offer You my broken life and my many sins. I believe that You died for them. I accept Your forgiveness and Your full pardon, and I ask that You wash me with Your Word. Help me to know the fullness of my relationship with You. Amen.

DAY 2
Old Scars

NEW FORGIVENESS...

"Blessed are the merciful:
for they shall obtain mercy."

MATTHEW 5:7

On our first date, we sat outside on a beautiful moonlit night. The night breeze cooled the warmth of summer. We talked for hours. I shared things that I had never shared with anyone else. I told him about my abusive stepfather whom I absolutely hated. As I spoke about him, my hatred became so venomous that it seemed to energize my words.

He was a good listener, but at this point he interrupted me: "You need to pray and ask God to show you how to forgive your stepfather."

That was almost 30 years ago, and until he said that I did not know that my inability to forgive my stepfather had caused me to become hard and cynical. I was unaware that because I harbored such unforgiveness I was the one who suffered the most. The memory of the offense and my attitude of unforgiveness were weighing me down.

APPLICATION

The ultimate example of mercy is the incarnation of Jesus. God literally got inside human skin, lived life as one of us, and then died for us. Mercy requires that we understand someone who has wronged us and why the person hurt us. When we forgive, we are cleansed and healed, and often the relationship is restored.

Is there a situation in your life that needs forgiveness? Learning how to move beyond the grip of unforgiveness and into a life of mercy and love requires patience, time, and conscious effort. The bible tells us to seek godly counsel in times of trouble. Make an appointment today to meet with a counselor at your church or ask your pastor to talk and pray with you. Understand that your progress may take time, but it will have an eternal impact.

PRAYER

Lord Jesus, I am a recipient of Your forgiveness based on Your shed blood on Calvary. Because of that forgiveness, I can come to You in prayer. I confess my sin of unforgiveness and ask for Your mercy. Show me how to move forward in forgiveness. Lead me in Your way, and I will follow in obedience. Amen.

DAY 3

Bearing All Things

LOVE AS JESUS DOES...

"[Love] beareth all things, believeth all things, hopeth all things, endureth all things."

1 CORINTHIANS 13:7

Clara laughed loudly as she spoke with friends after church, describing an outfit that could only belong to Aleta, who backed away as she realized that Clara was talking about her. The blood rushed to Aleta's face as she quickly got to her car in the church parking lot and let the tears flow. She thought Clara was a friend, and she was a member of the same prayer group. What should she do? Should she tell Clara that she was hurt by the remarks, or should she act like she hadn't overheard the insults? And how would that be

possible? As she went back and forth trying to decide what to do, she realized that her car wasn't starting. She looked up and saw Clara heading in her direction. Aleta knew that God wanted her to share her feelings and trust Him with the outcome.

APPLICATION

Scripture clearly teaches that when someone has offended us, it is our responsibility to approach the person about the offense in order to restore the relationship. Apostle Paul instructs the Corinthian believers on this subject when he says, "Love bears all things" (1 Corinthians 13:7). The Greek word here, stego, means to cover closely in order to keep liquid within a container; to shelter, protect, or endure without complaint. This literally means that when someone hurts or offends us, we are to protect the offender from exposure.

Forgiveness begins with an informed choice. Locate a few Scriptures whose focus is restoration of a relationship. Study these Scriptures and take notes on how to go about substantive forgiveness. Ask God to help you make an informed, protective choice about the person who offended you. As Christians, we already bear Christ's name; now we must bear His forgiving nature in our relationships.

PRAYER

Lord Jesus, thank You for bearing with me. You have protected me from exposure and ridicule. Help me to treat my enemy with grace and kindness. Show me how to speak well of the person and become his or her encourager. Amen.

DAY 4

Forgiveness Lasts

IT'S FOR THE LONG HAUL...

*"[Love]...hopeth all things,
endureth all things."*
1 CORINTHIANS 13:7B

Evelyn sat at her picture window and gazed across the street, lost in her thoughts. She looked over her shoulder at Raymond, napping on the sofa. She smiled slightly as she thought back over their 40-year marriage.

In the beginning, they had fought often. She was a Christian and tried to convince him—the unbeliever—that Christ was real. Raymond had cursed her and even prevented her from going to church sometimes. But she remained with him, even though she wondered how she could keep forgiving him for his verbal abuse and his efforts to stop her from believing in the Lord. More than once she almost divorced him, but a voice inside her constrained her, encouraging her to keep praying, forgiving, believing.

Then one Sunday, as she sat in the sanctuary focused on the message, the invitation to accept Christ was given. She became aware of stirrings around her as people glanced in her direction. Then she watched as Raymond went forward, accepted Christ, and thanked God for his godly wife, who loved him, never condemned him, and forgave him over and over again. That was 10 wonderful years ago, but Evelyn still remembered it as if it were yesterday.

APPLICATION

Paul writes to the Corinthian believers, "Love hopes all things [and] endures all things" because even when someone's misbehavior shatters our belief in goodness or repentance, love still hopes. As long as God's grace is operative, human failure is never final. We receive God's limitless grace, so we are required to extend that same grace to others.

Maybe you are in a long-term relationship and are ready to give up on it. If abusiveness characterizes the relationship, know that God has your safety in mind. Seek professional help from your pastor or others in your community. Meanwhile, cling to God's Word as an anchor and hold on for dear life. If you have an unbelieving spouse or loved ones, seek out other Christian women to share your burden. You will gain strength from their testimonies.

P R A Y E R

Lord God, I need You to help me renew my desire to hold onto Your love. I praise You that You never gave up on me. Show me how to forgive and love in a way that heals and restores joy. Amen.

DAY 5

An Unthinkable Forgiveness

FORGIVING THE UNFORGIVABLE...

"And be ye kind one to another, tenderhearted, forgiving one another, even as God for Christ's sake hath forgiven you."

EPHESIANS 4:32

In Southern California in the 1980s, a young girl was abducted, molested, and murdered. Her attacker was convicted and given a life sentence. The girl's grieving mother quit her job and moved from city to city, unable to find peace. Finally, she accepted a friend's invitation to go to church. Eventually, she accepted God's grace; and about

141

four years later, the memory of her daughter's life began to bring joy to her again. Memories of the killer began to soften, and she acknowledged his humanity.

She talked about forgiveness to other parents of victims—and even to offenders in prison. One day, as she shared her story at a prison, she heard herself saying, "My greatest desire is to forgive the man who crushed the life out of my daughter. In the name of Christ, I want him to feel loved and prized as a human being." Through her tears, she saw an inmate walk toward her.

"I am that man!" he exclaimed. They embraced in forgiveness.

APPLICATION

True forgiveness features reconciliation and a restored relationship. The greatest example of this involves God's pursuit of reconciliation with humanity. When we are born again, the Holy Spirit literally comes to abide within us. Within us, therefore, resides the full range and depth of forgiveness, reconciliation, and restoration. In the Lord alone lies our strength to take leave of desires to exact revenge. With Christ, we have the light of hope for healing damaged lives and restoring broken relationships.

Sit in a private, quiet space and be alone with God. This may well involve some strong emotions that emerge, so have items of comfort with you, such as a cup of herbal tea and a pillow to hug. Assure yourself that nothing—no situation, no difficulty—is too hard for God; He will ease your pain if you give Him a chance to do so. Go to God in prayer and confess the sin of unforgiveness. Seek God's wisdom for the appropriate steps in reaching out to the person who hurt you. Continue having this time with God as you undergo the process of forgiveness, reconciliation, and restoration.

PRAYER

Lord, this task is too hard for me to handle alone. I confess the sin of unforgiveness. Help me to see my offender as You see him. Help me to know the measure of Your love for him and to see the wonderful plan You have for his life. Then help me love and forgive him with Your love. Amen.

AUGUST
WEEK ONE: THE RIGHTEOUSNESS OF GOD

DAY 1

Worry Like A Thief

ROBBED OF GOD'S GIFT OF JOY...

*"He shall pray unto God,
and he will be favourable unto him:
and he shall see his face with joy:
for he will render unto man his righteousness."*

JOB 33:26

How many times have we awakened with a million and one things on our minds? Even though we say we believe that God will help us through moments of difficulty or uncertainty, we let our worries keep us awake, pursuing answers without seeking God's help. We neglect the solid assurance of Bible study and prayer, and the support we could have acquired from God takes

a back seat. As Job 33:26 points out, if we would pray to God—communicate about our worries and concerns—He will deliver to us His righteous ways of handling our dilemmas.

APPLICATION

For our worries about family, husband, friends, children, jobs, and so on, prayer is the most important solution because in prayer we deepen our relationship with God. Through prayer, we learn how to implement God's ways of righteous (moral) living. When we become weak, we cannot fight effectively and we are guilty of letting the thief in. He can only do this if we forget to pray and thus do not put on the righteousness of God.

Make a list right now of the things that are worrying you, and then give them to God in prayer.

PRAYER

Lord God, our eternal Father, thank You for Your righteousness. Thank You for letting us cast our cares upon You. Let us remember how to keep our joy. Lord, let us never forget that we can do nothing without you, but because of the Christ that lives within us we can do all things. Amen.

DAY 2

Right Standing with god

WHAT EQUIPMENT DO YOU NEED?

"Even the righteousness of God which is by faith of Jesus Christ unto all and upon all them that believe: for there is no difference."

ROMANS 3:22

Two sisters want to take a trip across a lake in a boat. They get into the boat, and they immediately begin to talk about what is required to be in right standing with God. We will call them Sister #1 and Sister #2. Let's listen in on their conversation.

Sister #1: We have been attending church since we were very young, and we have been faithful churchgoers all our lives. We certainly know right from wrong. We read our Bibles every day. We do unto others as we would have them do unto us.

Sister #2: We also witness to those who are lost. We give to the poor, we behave well, and most importantly we love the Lord.

They continue to talk about the things that they do for the Lord. Because of their consistency in doing these things, they are sure that they are in right standing with God.

Then the sisters realize that they have been out on the lake most of the day, but they haven't gotten anywhere. They begin to wonder why and then realize that they forgot their oars! Without the oars, those sisters weren't going to reach their destination.

APPLICATION

Our good works don't get us anywhere by themselves. We won't experience a sense of progress in our relationship with God if we've left our "oars" behind. In other words, misconceptions of what's required to be in right standing with God can waylay our walk with the Lord. God's righteousness is available to us, and it is not based on how often we attend church, get praised for participation in Bible study discussions, or anything else that passes favor. Even if we do all these things really well, we will still fail because we are human. We must possess two attributes to move along in our relationship with God: faith and belief. God's righteousness is by faith in Jesus Christ and bestowed upon all who believe (Romans 3:22).

Ask a trusted friend who is born again or an elder at your church to give you some suggestions as to how you can improve the progress of your relationship with God. Have a prayer circle about faith and belief and how these attributes are authentically displayed in everyday life.

PRAYER

Lord, we desire Your righteousness. Let us be willing to learn of You and to know what is required to obtain Your righteousness. Let us believe in Your Word. Amen.

DAY 3

Establishment in Righteousness

ASSURANCE AND PEACE...

"In righteousness shalt thou be established:
thou shalt be far from oppression; for thou shalt not fear:
and from terror; for it shall not come near thee."

ISAIAH 54:14

We need to be conscious of what righteousness means for us now and eternally. In Isaiah 54, we read that rejoicing is in store for us because God's offer of a proper way of life can free us from the terror of unbelief and uncertainty. We have no more reason to fear the enemy's oppressive ways of making us think we're unworthy of love, compassion, and confidence in our abilities. God establishes His righteous ways of living and treating one another because the Crucifixion made the way for us to come into right standing with God. Being established in righteousness directly impacts our lives forever.

When we have faith and believe in God, we are cleansed by the blood of Jesus Christ and sanctified with His Spirit. Once this is accomplished, we become new creatures and we are known in heaven as the righteousness of God. When things occur that would upset the average person, we will walk in righteousness with assurance and we will have peace. We might bend, but we will not break.

APPLICATION

Think through a recent situation that upset you a great deal. Did you have the peace of God in that situation? If not, why not? How could you have handled it differently?

PRAYER

Lord God, continue to remind us that in the establishment of Your righteousness comes assurance and peace in all situations. Remind us of our newness in You, and help us acquire attributes of faith and belief in You so we might acknowledge that our lives are changed forever because of the shedding of Your precious blood. Amen.

DAY 4

Our Sin for His Righteousness

WE MADE A GOOD TRADE ...

"For he hath made him to be sin for us, who knew no sin; that we might be made the righteousness of God in him."

2 CORINTHIANS 5:21

Sarah took a seat in the last pew. She could hear the pastor preaching, but she could not understand some of the words. She guessed she was still hung over from last night. Going out partying, dancing, smoking, drinking, and fornicating had become a normal routine for her. She wasn't sure, then, of exactly what drew her to the church today.

God's response was immediate and clear: Why not be here?

Suddenly Sarah found herself on her knees at the altar asking God to take away her sins. Sarah was saved that day and forevermore.

APPLICATION

Our sin was poured into Christ at His crucifixion. His righteousness is poured into us at our conversion. God trades His immeasurably precious righteousness for our worthless sin. This trade, to say the least, is uneven. Yet, it is absolutely necessary for us to have a chance at everlasting life. How grateful we should be; because without God's righteousness, we would surely perish.

Imagine that you possess an old item with high material value. You've saved the item for a long time, hoping you would have a child to pass it on to. But you never had a child. Now a neighbor's child visits you. He is dirty and sweaty and has bad manners, but he says he has something to trade with you. You decide to bestow the highly valuable item on him even though what he offers in trade is worthless. What will you tell the child to help him handle the trade well (righteously)? Consider how this analogy fits with your own treatment of God's bestowal of righteousness on you.

PRAYER

Lord God, thank You for this gift which cannot be measured. How grateful we are that You were willing to trade Your righteousness for our unworthiness. Lord, because of Your love of all people, each and every one of us has a chance to obtain eternal life. For this, we will forever praise and worship You. Amen.

DAY 5

Hungry And Thirsty?

THEN EAT AND DRINK...

"Blessed are they which do hunger and thirst after righteousness: for they shall be filled."

MATTHEW 5:6

The hunger after righteousness is seen in many of God's people in the Old and New Testaments (Psalm 42:1-2; 63:1; Philippians 3:10). All of God's children should fervently pray to know His ways, His heart, His purpose, His wisdom, His holy principles, and His suffering. In doing so, we come to know God Himself.

The Christian's hunger to learn and pass along God's attributes is often destroyed by worldly anxiety, the deceitfulness of riches, and the desire for things and worldly pleasure (Mark 4:19). But if believers' hunger for God and His righteousness is destroyed, we will die spiritually. For this reason, it is essential that we be sensitive to the Holy Spirit's convicting work in our lives (John 16:8-13).

The condition of one's spirit is similar to the condition of one's body. To stave off hunger pains, one must eat to control the hunger. To quench thirst, one must drink often. We are not going to satisfy these needs if we eat and drink only occasionally. Our health is dependent on the care we take to eat and drink properly. The condition of our spiritual person as well as our natural person will depend on how often we partake of food and beverage that benefit our spiritual and natural bodies. We should continually hunger for the presence of God and continually thirst for communion with Christ through His fellowship and the indwelling of the Holy Spirit.

APPLICATION

Each time you eat this week make a conscious effort to partake of His Word as well. Have a Bible with you at each meal and read a passage of Scripture. We should sit down at His table to eat and drink continuously.

PRAYER

Lord, You paid the price and we reap the benefits. We thank You for passing on Your instructions for righteous living and most of all for giving us Your blessings as we hunger and thirst for righteousness. Lord, let us know that Your food (the Word) will always satisfy us. We will not die spiritually because everything we need for our spiritual growth is in Your Word. Amen.

AUGUST
WEEK TWO: HOLINESS

DAY 1

Your Words Are Weapons

THE POWER OF POSITIVE WORDS...

"Death and life are in the power of the tongue: and they that love it shall eat the fruit thereof."

PROVERBS 18:21

Kathy had spent the last two months browsing through newspapers and Internet websites in her search for a new job. She'd been laid off from her clerk position at a law firm; and with gas, light, telephone, and mortgage bills stacked on top of the kitchen counter, Kathy considered the situation hopeless. As far as she was concerned, being a law clerk was a dream job she'd probably

never duplicate. Even though she called several companies to inquire about openings, she had little or no expectation of a positive response. She often hung up the phone and told herself, "I'll probably never hear from them again." Click!

APPLICATION

Before the foundation of the earth, God spoke to a mass of nothingness and said, "Let there be light." The light gleamed through darkness without any hesitation. God is so powerful that He spoke the world into existence in six days. His words were simply, "Let there be . . .!" Because we are children of the most high God, we inherit a measure of His power. We have the ability to speak life into a dead situation and watch it resurrect. Our words have the potential to determine our future. Do not hesitate to do it boldly.

During the hustle and bustle of your day, try turning every negative word into a positive one. If your boss, employee, or family member stirs up a negative statement, answer with a positive response that is edifying and uplifting. Regardless of how bad a situation may seem to your natural eye, speak life into it so you can pass on this transformative attribute.

PRAYER

Father God, through the power of Your Spirit, I pray that You would teach me how to look beyond the natural realm and speak the way You speak. In the name of Jesus, I pray. Amen.

DAY 2

The Lord's Temple

KEEPING IT HOLY...

*"I beseech you therefore, brethren,
by the mercies of God, that ye present your bodies
a living sacrifice, holy, acceptable unto God,
which is your reasonable service."*

ROMANS 12:1

Sharon had been celibate for five years, ever since she rededicated her life to Jesus Christ. After breaking up with her last boyfriend, she made a promise to God that she would no longer defile her body with a man that was not her husband. After faithfully remaining celibate and keeping herself busy with work and church activities, Sharon began to desire a romantic relationship. She often rented films filled with love scenes and listened to love songs that reminded her of past relationships. Soon, she was questioning her ability to remain celibate. Sharon was tired of waiting for God to send her a mate. She was ready to fulfill her own desires and wondered how much longer God expected her to keep herself holy.

APPLICATION

Sexual sin (fornication) is an act that is against God and also against one's own body. In 1 Corinthians 6:18, the Bible says to flee fornication. The Lord is telling His people to run the other way. Because we are vessels of God, the Lord expects us to use our bodies for His glory. Be honest with God about your weakness. Lean on Jesus for the strength to get through your trial. Fight the attitudes that erode your strength, such as impatience, frustration, or curiosity. Do not forget that you are a victorious woman of God who has been bought at a price. Allow Him to reside in you, in a place of sanctification and holiness, for He is holy.

Find a Scripture or song that gives you strength and hide it in your heart. When confronted with an enticing thought, recite your chosen Scripture or sing your song. Repeat the words of strength over and over again. Allow them to build you up.

PRAYER

Father, I thank You for creating me to be a victorious woman of God. Lord, help me to see myself as You see me. Give me the strength to please You with my body by keeping it holy. Purify me, O Lord, for Your glory. In the name of Jesus, I pray. Amen.

DAY 3

Keeping My Mind Stayed On You

FOCUSING THOUGHTS...

*"Set your affection on things above,
not on things on the earth."*

COLOSSIANS 3:2

Megan sat in a meeting at work on Thursday morning twiddling her thumbs. Her mind was consumed with things she didn't have. With less than eight days left before her 36th birthday, she wondered why she wasn't married, had no children, lived in a small one-bedroom apartment, and struggled to pay her bills on time each month. She no longer owned a car and couldn't see when she'd be able to afford another one. Feeling sorry for herself, she made an excuse about a bad headache and went home early. She ate a carton of chocolate ice cream and got into bed, hoping she'd fall asleep and forget she existed.

APPLICATION

Every action in which we indulge begins in our minds as a thought or an idea. The Bible states in Philippians 4:6-7, "Be anxious for nothing, but in everything by prayer and supplication, with thanksgiving, let your requests be made known to God; and the peace of God, which surpasses all understanding, will guard your hearts and minds through Christ Jesus" (NKJV). We are exhorted in this passage not to worry about anything, but to give every aspect of our lives over to God through prayer and faith.

As women of God, we must strive to keep our minds focused on the kingdom of heaven. Still, it can be challenging to think on the things of Christ consistently for long periods of time. When a thought or panic attack occurs, take a moment and write it down on a small piece of paper. Read it aloud and ask yourself: Is this situation too hard for my God to work out? Your answer will be a definite no! Lift the small paper in the air and give it to God. Whatever you wrote the paper no longer belongs to you. It's God's.

PRAYER

Lord, I need You to consume every thought in my mind that is not of You. Lord, You have dominion and power over every situation in my life. Replace my faithless thoughts with trust and hope. I believe You have already worked out everything. In the name of Jesus, I pray. Amen.

DAY 4
Matters of the Heart

HOW GOOD IS GOOD ENOUGH?

*"With my whole heart have I sought thee:
O let me not wander from thy commandments.
Thy word have I hid in mine heart,
that I might not sin against thee."*
PSALM 119:10-11

Carol attended church every Sunday, arrived at work on time every day, and lived a simple life. She casually read her Bible twice a week, only gossiped on the telephone about her coworkers after a rumor had already started, uttered a curse word only when a car cut her off on the road, and committed fornication once every six months when her ex-boyfriend was in town. Her philosophy regarding her lifestyle was: "Nobody's perfect."

APPLICATION

Becoming complacent with God can be dangerous. When we casually regard some sins as less important than other sins, we grieve God's Spirit. Our faith in the Lord Jesus Christ is not based on regular attendance in church. The real measure of holiness is based on how we conduct ourselves every day and in every place. The Lord wants His children to regard every sin as being just as grotesque as He does. We must search and study the Scriptures earnestly and allow God to purify us from every unclean thing in our lives.

Take one whole day to evaluate yourself. Ask yourself if God would be pleased with your attitude, words, and actions. Trust the Holy Spirit to give you the answer. If the Spirit of God says no, begin making wholesome changes. Be sensitive to the leading of the Holy Spirit as you seek the answers.

PRAYER

Lord, it is my desire to be more like You. Father, show me all of my ways that are not pleasing in Your sight. Reveal what holiness looks like so that I may glorify You in every aspect of my lifestyle. Lord, where I have stumbled, forgive me. Allow Your Spirit to convict me in the areas that need to be purified. In Jesus' name, I pray. Amen.

DAY 5

Where The Spirit is, There Is Liberty

GAINING DISCERNMENT...

*"Howbeit when he, the Spirit of truth,
is come, he will guide you into all truth:
for he shall not speak of himself;
but whatsoever he shall hear, that shall he speak:
and he will shew you things to come."*

JOHN 16:13

Denise Howard had been pastor of a small church in the Midwest for two years. She often relied on the counsel of the board, elders, deacons, and trustees to help make decisions regarding business matters of the church. Because this was her first pastorate, she left it to these leaders to make decisions with the church's best interests in mind. One day, the deacons, trustees, and the rest of the group approached her regarding a new program they wanted to implement for the singles ministry. Immediately, Pastor Howard's spirit did not agree with the new idea. But they already had put it in motion.

APPLICATION

When Jesus Christ ascended to the heavens after His glorious resurrection, He made it known that He would leave us a Comforter that would guide us into all truth. The Comforter would indeed live in every born-again believer. Because of this great gift, we have access to wisdom, knowledge, and prophetic information. We are mandated to follow the leading of the Holy Spirit. God has the map of our lives in His hands. He knows what is ahead, regardless of how a situation looks in the natural realm. Trust the revelation that you hear in the depths of your spirit when faced with a proposal. If you are attuned to God, you will know the truthful response. Where there is truth, there is freedom. Glory to God!

Take a few moments out of your day and give God the highest praise. Tell Him how awesome He is. Thank Him for giving you the Holy Spirit. Thank Him for being the great I AM. Lift your hands to Him and speak about His majesty.

PRAYER

Lord, I thank You for the power of Your Spirit. I thank You for bringing revelation when I need it most. Father, teach me to walk in the truth and holiness of Your Word. I ask that You would give me the gift of discernment so that I might know Your will. In Jesus' name, I pray. Amen.

AUGUST
WEEK THREE: MINISTRY

DAY 1

We Have This Ministry

WHO, ME IN MINISTRY?

"Therefore seeing we have this ministry, as we have received mercy, we faint not."

2 CORINTHIANS 4:1

The small room was filled with ladies saying what they wanted to get out of the new Bible study class. Several expressed a desire just to learn more about the Bible. Kathy said she was uncomfortable standing before a group and talking; she preferred studying the Bible on her own but recognized the class might be helpful.

One of the other ladies said, "I don't know if I am supposed to have a ministry."

These ladies were wives, single parents, grandmothers, aunts, and women with busy careers. Overall, their statements reflected timidity, fear, unworthiness, and lack of confidence and training. The teacher told the class that many Christian women have shortsighted views of themselves and don't see their potential for ministry.

But the teacher, Sis Davis, shared that God has called each woman and gifted her with a special gift for ministry. Each woman has the opportunity for her own ministry: sharing the truth of the Gospel. How and to whom she does so is part of her life's journey.

APPLICATION

Some women feel excluded or think that ministry is only for those in the pulpit, wearing a robe and standing before a congregation, or otherwise possessing expertise. Women everywhere, in all walks of life and on every spiritual level of growth, need to know that true opportunities for ministry exist all around. The person with the gift of ministry has a servant's heart. She will see opportunities to be of service and seize them. We are members in one body and members of one another with many gifts to edify the body (Romans 12:5).

Write down all the services you render and how God can verify areas of ministry in your life.

PRAYER

Dear Father, open my mind and heart to new areas of ministry that You have for me. Help me to understand Your plan and purpose for the ministry You have purposed for my life. In Jesus' name. Amen.

DAY 2

Ministry of Reconciliation

RESTORING BROKEN VESSELS...

*"And all things are of God, who hath reconciled
us to himself by Jesus Christ, and hath given to us
the ministry of reconciliation; To wit,
that God was in Christ, reconciling the world unto himself,
not imputing their trespasses unto them;
and hath committed unto us the word of reconciliation.
Now then we are ambassadors for Christ,
as though God did beseech you by us:
we pray you in Christ's stead, be ye reconciled to God."*

2 CORINTHIANS 5:18-20

Thomas and Betty answered the call to serve
God in the inner city of Chicago. With their
two young sons, they moved into a high crime

179

area and opened a community center. They had little money, but they had faith in God. Thomas and Betty started by visiting people's homes and inviting kids to come to the center. Other Christians saw their vision and began to join the couple for outreach training and door-to-door evangelism. Even though they sometimes had mixed feelings about her safety and mixed responses from people in the neighborhood, in time Betty and Thomas witnessed people's yearning to know God.

Soon many children, teens, and adults were coming to know Jesus Christ through the daring ministry of reconciliation. As other Christians spread the ministry of reconciliation in their community, people were reconciled to God and their lives were changed. Families were united. The youth grew and developed maturity through the Gospel, and many Christians rose to the challenge and received training in evangelism.

APPLICATION

In today's Scripture, we read that we who have been reconciled to God have been given the ministry of reconciliation—bringing people to Christ and discipling them for growth. Through effective evangelism and discipleship, we become ambassadors for Christ, pleading with men and women to reconcile themselves to God.

Wherever you go, you will find opportunities to be an ambassador for Christ—to represent Him well and share the Gospel. Today, look for your opportunity to act on your ministry of reconciliation and represent your Savior well!

❧

PRAYER

Lord, thank You for providing the many opportunities for me to minister to people. Help me to remember Your words in the Great Commission (Matthew 28:18-19). You have given me the ministry of reconciliation, the ministry of bringing people to You. In Jesus' name. Amen.

DAY 3
Ministry of my Home
FROM A MESS TO A MINISTRY...

"Every wise woman buildeth her house:
but the foolish plucketh it down with her hands."
PROVERBS 14:1

Jackie had three children tugging at her every moment. They kept her busy with cleaning, cooking, homework supervision, and all the other never-ending tasks of mother, wife, and woman. Jackie had completed college, married, and envisioned an enjoyable career with a wonderful husband, beautiful home, and lots of entertaining of family and friends. But now she felt trapped by her responsibilities. When her husband arrived home from work, she wanted to look nice, have

dinner ready and the house orderly, but she rarely managed to do this. The house was always a mess so they didn't host any functions with friends or family.

Jackie felt crushed. She wanted so badly for her home to be a place of ministry for her husband, her children, and others. As a Christian witness, she knew she needed help. She sought a godly older woman for counsel.

APPLICATION

In the Scripture, we are advised that the wise woman builds her house, but the foolish plucks it down with her own hands. The woman who works at building her house (her family and her life in addition to her home) is a virtuous, wise woman who knows God. Her husband can trust her because she will do him good. She works willingly. She is discreet in her spending and selective in her buying. She plans ahead so that her family is prepared. She takes care of herself and this can mean that she delegates some tasks. Her speech contains words of kindness and wisdom. She looks after the needs of her family. Her secret to success is her fear of the Lord, which is the beginning of wisdom.

Take stock of your home—the people, the place, and how you spend your time. Be honest in your inventory. It may require some restructuring of time or budget to turn your home into a place that demonstrates your love of God and becomes a favorite place for family and friends, love and laughter.

∿

PRAYER

Lord, thank You for my home and for those around me, including my neighbors and my community. Let me see the needs of my family as opportunities for ministry. Help my attitude to become that of the wise woman who builds. In Jesus' name. Amen.

DAY 4

Ministry of Intercession

HELP LORD, MY FRIEND NEEDS YOU...

"I exhort therefore, that, first of all, supplications, prayers, intercessions, and giving of thanks, be made for all men."

1 TIMOTHY 2:1

Dorothy was in her senior years and was feeling useless. As a single parent, she had raised her only son, who died when he was 35. She then helped raise her grandchildren. She took them to church and Sunday school to help them learn more about Jesus. She prayed for her grandchildren and later her great-grandchildren as they were born.

When Dorothy's 72nd birthday arrived, she retired and had more time on her hands. She wanted to do more for the Lord. As she sought the Lord, people began to call her with their prayer requests. Young people began to ask her to pray for them. God began to burden her heart to use her time to pray for others.

Today, at age 80, Dorothy has a prayer ministry around the world as she prays for missionaries, pastors, families, her country, and its government. She prays for schools. She clips out articles from the news media, church bulletins, and letters and prays for the various needs. She conducts a prayer line locally and nationally and has an effective ministry of intercession, coordinating a team to pray during church services. She no longer feels useless.

APPLICATION

In the Scripture, we are challenged to pray. Supplications, prayers and intercessions, and giving of thanks are to be made for all people. The ministry of intercessory prayer is available to anyone. There is no open glory, but it is a high and holy privilege to stand in the gap and pray for others. It's a front line position in spiritual warfare, pulling down strongholds and battling everything that exalts itself against the knowledge of God (2 Corinthians 10:4-5).

Start a prayer journal and record the miracles God will do through your prayers. As you grow in your acquaintanceship with prayer, let others know that you will pray for them and allow them to give you their prayer requests. If we are faithful in the little things, He will make us ruler over much more.

PRAYER

Lord, make me an intercessor for Thee. Help me to be faithful as an intercessor in this high and holy calling. In Jesus' name. Amen.

DAY 5

Ministry to the Lord

ANOINTING JESUS?

"And being in Bethany in the house of Simon the leper, as he sat at meat, there came a woman having an alabaster box of ointment of spikenard very precious; and she brake the box, and poured it on his head."

MARK 14:3

Brenda had seen it all. By the age of 45, she had experienced a wild and rough life. As a rebellious teen, she started using drugs and selling her body to support her habit. Sadly, by age 25, Brenda had had three abortions and was filled with guilt. She had also given birth to a son

that was put up for adoption, and she never saw him again. Her guilt contributed to her drinking habit. Her family rejected her because of her lifestyle.

Now she was tired of her reckless, wild lifestyle and did not want it to continue. After a nearly successful suicide attempt, she wound up in the hospital. While there a staff member witnessed to her, and she came to her senses and accepted the Lord. With such a broken and battered life, she wondered what she could offer. She opened up to the Lord and said, "Lord, I offer You my all...my brokenness. I want to worship You with my whole heart. Take what's left. It's Yours."

APPLICATION

In the Scripture, we see Mary of Bethany who had been forgiven much by Jesus. He would soon be crucified and buried. Because of her love for the Savior, she took spikenard, a very precious and costly ointment, and poured the ointment on Jesus. When the people spoke against her actions, Jesus spoke up for her. When we offer our best to Jesus, He accepts our offering of praise and worship. Others may find fault because they do not know our hearts. But God knows when you have done what you could in your ministry to Him.

Today, think of ways that you can give praise and worship to the Lord. Be expansive in your thinking. God delights in the praises of His children. He is more than worthy of all praise, honor, and glory. Take some extra time to worship and adore Him.

PRAYER

Lord, if I have been too busy for time with You, I ask forgiveness. I worship You and offer praises to You. Other things can wait while I linger in Your presence and am renewed. Let my praise be a sweet-smelling aroma to You. In Jesus' name. Amen.

AUGUST
WEEK FOUR: WITNESSING

DAY 1
When You Can See God's Hand

TELLING OTHERS HOW GOD HAS WORKED...

"Behold, the Lord's hand is not shortened, that it cannot save; neither his ear heavy, that it cannot hear."

ISAIAH 59:1

At a young age, Carolyn married Clarence, giving up her dream of becoming a nurse to be a housewife and then mother to their two children. Even though Clarence was verbally abusive, he was a doctor and a good financial provider; and she felt that made up for his abusiveness. She thought many times about leaving during their 18-year marriage, but she took her vows seriously.

Carolyn noticed that Clarence was away from home a lot. Her woman's intuition told her that he was having an affair, and sure enough he was. Carolyn suggested that they go to counseling, but Clarence refused. He filed for divorce and gave her just enough money to maintain the house and provide basic child support.

After a period of deep depression, Carolyn began to recover. A best friend reminded her of her dream of becoming a nurse. Carolyn got a job at a local mall, went to school at night, started back to church, and rededicated her life to God. Times were tough, but she kept going. She put both kids through college, got her degree in nursing, and became the head nurse in a hospital operating room. She thought that she needed Clarence, but God showed her that what she really needed was God. Now Carolyn tells everyone she meets about God's hand in her life and the difference this made when she had given up hope.

APPLICATION

The Bible tells us that if we delight ourselves in the Lord, He will give us the desires of our heart (Psalm 37:4). Never put your hope in the wrong thing. Give yourself only to God because His design for your life requires that you allow the unfolding to occur. He will then give you opportunities to tell others about what God has done for you.

What dream has God helped you to fulfill? Identify it, turn it into a testimony, and begin to tell others.

PRAYER

God, I ask You to help me develop courage so that I may be able to face life's challenges. Show me that I am a divine instrument and that Your hand is at work in my life. Give me the courage to share my experiences. Amen.

DAY 2
Witnessing to the Broken-Hearted

LOOK AROUND AND SEE THE PAIN...

ove the Lord, all ye his saints: for the Lord preserveth the faithful, d plentifully rewardeth the proud doer. Be of good courage, and he shall strengthen your heart, all ye that hope in the Lord."

PSALM 31:23-24

Lisa and John adored each other. One week, John went out of town on business. As he was driving back, he phoned Lisa and asked her to meet him at his home in 30 minutes. Lisa was excited. She missed him terribly. She went to his home, let herself in, and waited and waited. Two hours later, two policemen informed her that John had been killed in an accident.

Lisa felt terrible. She had been depressed for over a year when someone at work invited her to come to church. There she found loving people, people who had also suffered great losses and people who knew God. She came to know God, too. One particular friend, Allison, started calling Lisa on weekends and going out for coffee with her. Allison didn't pretend to know what Lisa was going through, but her presence helped. Lisa's depression began to lift.

One night, she had a dream that John came to her and said, "Lisa, honey, you must go on—you must live." She awakened and immediately prayed to God to mend her broken heart. Once Lisa allowed God and His people to come into her life, she learned how to love again. She also witnessed at her church so others could hear about God's presence in her life.

APPLICATION

Loss is common. Some have lost children, spouses, friends, parents, siblings. Wherever you go and whatever you do, chances are that you will come across someone who is trying to cope with loss. Think about your friends, coworkers, and neighbors. Which ones have recently suffered loss? Express your sympathy to that person in a quiet way and offer to pray for him or her, or invite the person to church. Tell them about God! Tell them about the Father who lost His only Child. Tell them that God can fill the huge hole left by the loss of that person. If you have not suffered great loss, do not assert that you know how this person is feeling. Chances are you don't. But listen, be present, and do not be put off by their emotions. Bless them and show them the way to God.

PRAYER

Lord, I ask that You give me insight to see the sorrows carried by those around me. In their dark times, let me point them to Your light. Amen.

DAY 3

Witnessing Through Financial Strain

GOD WILL PROVIDE...

*"Give, and it shall be given unto you; good measure, pressed down, and shaken together, and running over, shall men give into your bosom.
For with the same measure that ye mete withal it shall be measured to you again."*

LUKE 6:38

Pam was a dedicated employee, eager to take on new challenges and always willing to help coworkers. One morning while on her way to work, her car was rear-ended; she suffered a broken leg and a pinched nerve in her neck. She notified her employer about the accident and

the doctors' requirement that she stay home and undergo extensive physical therapy. But when doctors gave her permission to return to work, her employer sent her a letter stating that she no longer had a position. She was devastated. It was not her fault that she was injured in a car accident, and now a job she had enjoyed and did well was gone.

Times got hard for Pam. Bills piled up. She turned to the only source she knew: God. Each day Pam prayed to God for a financial blessing to pay her bills, and she thanked God in advance because she knew that God would supply all her needs. The entire time that Pam was out of work, God paid her bills. In fact, whenever she had extra money, she used it to bless someone else and told the person how God provided for her. Now that God has blessed Pam with a better job, she continues to bless others. She gets great joy from telling others how God met her needs during a challenging time.

APPLICATION

Woman of God, you know that God has been a blessing to you in good times and in bad; it's imperative that you be a blessing to someone else. Bless others when they are in financial need. Take someone to dinner. Pay a bill for someone. Slip some cash into a laid-off friend's purse. Talk to a creditor on someone's behalf. Drop off a bag filled with toiletries for a hard-hit, elderly neighbor. Pray with people whose financial struggles are burdensome, believing that God will meet their needs. Also, enlist other members of the body of Christ to pray for others and help them in concrete ways.

PRAYER

Today, God, help me to notice the blessings in every area of my life. And help me to be a blessing in someone else's life. You will provide. Amen.

DAY 4
Witnessing After a Crisis
FIGHTING CANCER WITH FAITH...

*"For she said within herself,
If I may but touch his garment, I shall be whole."*
MATTHEW 9:21

While Laverne was taking a shower one day, she did her monthly breast exam and noticed a lump in her right breast. She knew this was nothing to ignore and saw her ob-gyn doctor right away. The doctor also felt the lump, and soon afterward a surgeon discovered that Laverne had breast cancer.

Laverne, an otherwise healthy 30-year-old woman was in shock, but she moved forward anyway with a proactive response. She had a lumpectomy, chemotherapy treatments, and radiation. Even though she lost her hair, she refused to wear a wig because she had nothing to be ashamed of. She was determined not to allow breast cancer to attack her womanhood. She was also determined not to allow breast cancer to defeat her. Most importantly, she knew that God was in control of her life, and she loved telling other cancer patients about His unconditional love.

APPLICATION

Many people are afraid of cancer; but cancer does not always mean an immediate death sentence, and during times of affliction God can reveal Himself as the ultimate Healer. God gives us the power to speak life to any seemingly dead situation.

Take better care of yourself. Do a monthly breast exam, and get a yearly physical that includes a pap smear and a mammography test. Encourage other women to do the same. Be a witness on behalf of the importance of good self-care by talking to someone today about the great gift that your body is from God and the value of cherishing God's gift with regular caretaking. Speak life today to those who are medically suffering.

PRAYER

Lord, I trust in Your divine plan, and I know You know what is best for me. I thank You for the body that is so fearfully and wonderfully made. Keep me healthy, Lord. When I am not healthy, help me to affirm my belief in You and Your providence. Help me to encourage others during their quests for good health. Amen.

❦

DAY 5

Witnessing Through Faithfulness

GOD SEES US THROUGH TRIALS...

"Therefore being justified by faith,
we have peace with God through our Lord Jesus Christ:
By whom also we have access by faith into this grace
wherein we stand, and rejoice in hope of the glory of God.
And not only so, but we glory in tribulations also:
knowing that tribulation worketh patience."

ROMANS 5:1-3

One day in August, a huge flood swept through the city and people suffered great losses. The flood destroyed Stacey's home. She lost everything she owned. Many people questioned God, but not Stacey. Because of her faith and

strong religious upbringing, she began to praise God for just being alive. She had to move in with relatives, which was awkward at times. However, even though her worldly possessions were gone, she still found joy.

Stacey volunteered at a local Salvation Army site to help take her mind off her troubles and to help others. The stories they told and their determination to recover inspired her as she found herself encouraging those affected by the flood. She discovered that people were coming together in ways she hadn't noticed before the flood, learning how to give thanks in good times as well as bad.

APPLICATION

Blessed are the desperate for they shall find hope in Jesus Christ. Today, look back over your life and see where God has brought you. If you are facing trials, thank God for what you will learn. If those you know are encountering trials, listen to their stories and, if they haven't already done so, introduce them to Jesus, who can turn every trial into a blessing. If they are born again, join them in prayer. Be a witness of God's goodness so that others will be delivered, set free, and saved. Always remember that to whom much is given, much is required.

PRAYER

God, help me to recognize that misfortune is only temporary and from it we are drawn closer to You. Bring into my life those who need encouragement and a word of testimony during their trials. Amen.

KING JAMES VERSION

WOMEN of COLOR
STUDY BIBLE